CONVENTION AND REVOLT IN POETRY

CONVENTION AND REVOLT IN POETRY

BY

JOHN LIVINGSTON LOWES

Professor of English in Harvard University

BOSTON AND NEW YORK
HOUGHTON MIFFLIN COMPANY
The Riverside Press Cambridge

NINTH IMPRESSION, OCTOBER, 1931

TO
M. C. L.

PREFACE

A GOOD deal of water has run under the mill since this book was first published, a decade ago. It was the period then of the delighted emergence of the so-called "New Poetry" — a term as old, for a thing as old, as poetry itself — and conservatives and radicals were eagerly calling each other bitter names. It seemed worth while to essay the part of an unsolicitous spectator of the game, and to view a clash which was at once perennial and ephemeral in the light of considerations less personal and partisan than those which at the moment were being bandied back and forth. The attempt proved to be illuminating at least to the writer, and since the book, in the last ten years, has been frequently reprinted, it seems fair to assume that it may have been of use to others too. That is the warrant for once more reprinting it, this time in a more attractive form. Beyond the correction of errors, no changes have been made in the text. A newer New Poetry has, to be sure, already appeared, and yet newer will inevitably follow. But precisely that permanence in flux is the large and humane experience of Poetry — and that is the theme of the book.

The chapters which constitute it were delivered as lectures at the Lowell Institute in Boston during January, 1918. The last lecture grew, in part, out of what was then the one dominating and unescapable influence on all our thinking. It has been allowed to stand, as the *apologia pro vita sua* of such a book at such a time.

J. L. L.

26 *December*, 1929

CONTENTS

CONVENTION AND REVOLT IN POETRY

I

THE ROOTS OF CONVENTION

THE subject immediately before us is the roots of convention in poetry, not its beginnings. I have no intention of scrutinizing the dark backward and abysm of time for the dancing throng, or of disquieting the spirits of the ancient bards to bring them up. The origins of convention chronologically considered will not concern us here. There is, to be sure, keen zest in retracing the vestiges of primitive poetry, and in reconstructing, *ex pede Herculem*, primitive poetry itself. To build up Hercules from his foot, when everything above the ankle is your own creation, is an alluring exercise, and I confess its fascination, and yield to no one in my recognition of its fruitfulness. But I shall take another way. The phenomena of which I wish to speak spring from the very nature of poetry. In a word, it is because poetry is what it is that its conventions are what they are. And my task at the moment is the scrutiny of poetry itself. In the face of that enterprise I feel with Keats in one of his letters: "The Cliff of Poesy towers above me, [and] I am one that 'gathers Samphire, dreadful trade.'"

We may deal summarily with the definition of convention. I am speaking to you now. And I am using sounds which have not the remotest logical connection with the things for which they stand. They mean what they mean solely because we accept them as meaning it. "Horse" has no more connection with the animal it names than "ἵππος," or "equus," or "cheval," or "Pferd." The varying sounds convey the idea of the creature to their respective users simply because, through immemorial consent, they are so understood. That is one element in convention — *acceptance*. There is another. An artist sets to work to paint a landscape. But the landscape has three dimensions, the flat surface before him has but two. Out of the limitations of his medium he must construct a set of symbols that will give to a plane the appearance of depth. He does it, and we accept it, and see depth where it is not. A dramatist writes a play. The action covers days, weeks, perhaps months, or even years. The play-

wright has at his disposal a brief three hours.
Out of the limitations of his medium he must
somehow bring it about that stage time shall produce the impression of real time. We know that
hours and months do not synchronize, yet we
accept them as coincident; we know that a surface has only two dimensions, yet we accept it
as representing three. The major conventions of
/art, in other words, involve not only acceptance,
but acceptance of *illusion*.

/ We are dealing, then, with the communication
of ideas, perceptions, feelings, impressions. That
involves a medium. The medium and the thing
communicated do not correspond: stage time is
not real time, a surface has not depth, words are
not things. There are differences between the relations in each case, of course, but in all one fundamental fact appears: we accept as one thing
something which is another and a different thing.

Convention, therefore, so far as art is concerned, represents concurrence in certain accepted methods of communication. And the
fundamental conventions of every art grow out
of the nature of its medium. Conventions beget
conventions, to be sure, and their ramifications
and permutations are endless. But that, for the
moment, is another story. Our business now is

with the roots of conventions in poetry. What is the problem that the poet has to solve?

Here, on the one hand, is what William James once called "the blooming welter" — everything from a sea-shell to Chicago, from a restless gossamer to the swing of the planets, from my lady's eyebrow to the stuff of "Lear." And here is the poet who feels it all and strives to catch and fix it — to catch it and fix it in *words*. How shall he do it? Let me quote a part of Goethe's famous answer to those inquiring spirits who kept asking what idea he sought to embody in "Faust":

It was n't, on the whole, my way, as a poet, to strive after the embodiment of something abstract. I received within myself impressions — impressions of a hundred sorts, sensuous, lively, lovely, many-hued — as an alert imaginative energy presented them. And I had as a poet nothing else to do but mould and fashion within me such observations and impressions, and through a vivid representation to bring it about that others should receive the same impression, when what I had written was read or heard.

There we have it again in a nutshell: the phantasmagoria of the concrete world; the poet's mind like a sensitized film, alive to impressions; the impulse to give to these impressions form, and to communicate. But, once more, how? Since it is a poet of whom we're talking, his only medium is words. What happens? Let us assume a case.

I lie on the sand by the seashore. And there pour in on me a throng of physical sensations: light — gleaming and sparkling on the sea, shattered into fragments of a rainbow in the spindrift, glinting from the sand, glancing along the waving beach grass, luminous in the air; color — the infinite purples of the sea, a phantom ship shell-pink, the white flash of a gull; line — the pure, sharp line where sea meets sky, the curve of the beach, the exquisite pattern left by the receding waves; sound — the slow, recurrent, rhythmic thunder of the sea, the wind through the grass and in my ears, like Dante's voice within a voice; touch — the texture of the sand as I sift it through my fingers, the wind, soft and flowing across my body, the warmth of the sun felt beneath the wind; taste and smell — the fresh, salty tang of the sea. And those are but a moiety of the sum.

Now clearly there are two things to be reckoned with — I, and the surging mass of impressions. But what for the moment I call "I," is no less complex than what I've just sketched. I may, as I lie on the sand, be happy, dejected, in vacant or in pensive mood, alone and glad to be, alone and wishing that I were n't, in company that harmonizes, in company that jars. I may be seeing the ocean for the first time, returning to it after a long absence, renewing a daily pilgrimage. I may be steeped in all that the poets have ever sung about the sea, or my mind may be to it a *tabula rasa*. I may be caught by the sea's mystery, oppressed by its vastness, stirred by the majestic "Hitherto shalt thou come, but no further; and here shall thy proud waves be stayed." The I who see am as manifold as what I see, and what I see takes form and color, proportion and emphasis, from what I feel. It is obviously a problem of two worlds with which we have to deal. Heaven forbid that I should psychologize or metaphysicize. Call the two worlds, if you like, the subjective and the objective, the microcosm and the macrocosm — or any tag-words that will ticket them. What I want to make clear is a *situation* — a protean and multiform *ego* (I pay that homage to the psychologists) over against a rich and thronging world of sensible things. And out of that situation there arise (to use again words from a letter of Keats) "the innumerable compositions and decompositions which take place between the intellect and its thousand materials before it arrives at that trembling, del-

icate, and snail-horn perception of beauty,"
which emerges from the labyrinth.

But let us go one step further. Suppose I am a
poet, with the artist's imperious instinct to *express*. Two more elements enter in, my audience
and my medium. The audience is a bridge which
we shall cross when we come to it. And for a
poet, the sole medium is words. And there's the
rub.

For what we are concerned with is the communication of what is seen, felt, heard, tasted,
smelled. And once more the medium is speech.
But words cannot give the things in themselves.
Color can give color, line line, but the relation
between words and things is not and cannot be
direct. Words are not warm or luminous, they
have not line or color, they are not salt, they are
odorless. Sound and movement they have, in
common with what I hear and see, and that is all.
But even so, the sound and movement are not
the same. I cannot give the things directly; I
must transfer and translate. If I say the sea is
blue, the sea has a thousand blues. And the blue
off Nantucket is not the miracle of luminous,
translucent color off Sardinia. Once more, I cannot paint it; what do I do? I fall back upon its
relations to things that are like, yet different —

more fixed than it, less fluctuating, indeterminate, evanescent. "A . . . breeze, ruffling up the *larkspur-blue* sea, breaking the tops of the waves into *egg-white* foam, shoving ripple after ripple of pale *jade-green* over the shoals of Aboukir Bay"; "Blue as the tip of a deep blue salvia blossom, the inverted cup of the sky arches over the sea." Those are from a prose poem published a few months ago by the most modern of the modernists. We have not advanced a step (nor can we), so far as the inexorable limitations of the medium are concerned, beyond the "wine-dark sea" of Homer.

We are shut up, then, in our expression of the actual world as it impinges upon us, to indirections. "What does it look like, sound like, feel like, taste like, smell like?" — that formula is the very sea-mark of our utmost sail. Come back for a moment to our supposititious poet on the beach. How does he, in point of fact, translate his world of sea and sky? The flash and sparkle of the sunlit waves become Æschylus' "innumerable laughter" of Shakespeare's "multitudinous sea." The breakers "dart their hissing tongues high up the sand"; "the hard sand breaks, And the grains of it Are clear like wine"; "the low wind whispers near"; out on the ship, "the sails do sigh like sedge"; nearer, "the mighty Being is awake, And doth with his eternal motion make A sound like thunder everlastingly"; and by and by night "smokes about the burning crest Of the old, feeble, and day-wearied sun." We even turn the thing about:

> And through the music of the languid hours,
> They hear like ocean on a western beach
> The surge and thunder of the Odyssey.

I know I am talking of a trite and threadbare theme — namely, figures of speech. But the trite we fight shy of because it *is* trite, is sometimes more shining than the upstart new, if we will but brush off the dust. And we are apt to forget, in our boredom with the eternal truisms about similes and metaphors as poetical embellishments, the pregnant fact of the inevitability of imagery — an inevitability rooted and grounded as deeply in the nature of the poet's medium, language, as stage time is inherent in the necessities of the dramatic medium, or perspective in the restrictions of a flat surface. And the poet, strive as he may, cannot escape the limitations. Dorothy Wordsworth wrote in her "Journal" in 1802: "William tired himself with seeking an epithet for the cuckoo." And he tired himself, at intervals, for just forty-three years in the attempt to express directly what cannot be expressed directly — the sound of the cuckoo's "wandering voice." Read especially the second stanza of "To the Cuckoo," written in 1802, as Wordsworth came back and back to it in 1807, 1815, 1820, 1827, and 1845, and struggled between fact and seeming. Yet the final triumph of the poem — a triumph unsurpassed in its kind in English poetry — lies primarily in its translation of the cuckoo's literal voice into terms of inner experience.

Nor is the inevitability of imagery, of course, confined to verse. It belongs to every attempt to give in words our impression of things. Dorothy Wordsworth was, I suspect, a far more keen and exquisite observer than her brother. She puts in her "Journal" one day her favorite birch tree. How does she make us see what she sees? "The sun shone upon it, and it gleamed in the wind *like a flying, sunshiny shower*. It was a tree in shape, with stem and branches, but it was *like a spirit of water*." Fitzgerald, like our hypothetical poet, is basking in the sun: "Here is a glorious sunshiny day; all the morning I read about Nero in Tacitus, lying at full length on a bench in a garden; a nightingale singing, and some red anemones *eyeing the sun manfully* not far off."

"A funny mixture all this," he goes on: "Nero and the delicacy of spring . . . nightingales singing, [and] Tacitus full of pleasant atrocity." Well, the blooming welter *is* a funny mixture, in which, please observe, Fitzgerald himself is an essential element! And that brings us back from the world perceived to the other element in our complex: namely, the percipient poet — to me (who am obligingly playing the part), with my permanent bents, my transient emotions, my passing moods. For what I strive to give is, again, not the things themselves but my impression of things — things, that is, as they affect me, as I feel them.

But can I express even my feelings directly? I can say: "I am sad." But "sad" tells no more than "blue" before. There are as many sadnesses as there are shifting aspects of the sea. I can say: "I hate." But is it the hatred of Shylock for Antonio, or of Regan and Goneril for Cordelia, or of St. Paul for sin, or of Germany for England? I can say: "I love"; but the gradations and degrees of love are infinite. Is it the love of John, Peter, Paul, Martha, Mary, St. Francis, or St. Theresa, "with all her brim-filled bowls of fierce desire"? Is it the love of Launcelot, Tristan, Romeo, Anthony, Abelard, Dante,

Goethe, or of this óne or that of all the infinitely diverse men and women who have ever lived and loved, "even as you and I"? "I love," for telling all, is like saying, "the sea sounds."

᠎ I have, to be sure, a means of expressing my feelings directly. There are cries, tears, gestures, shining eyes, quivering nostrils, compressed lips. And the painters and sculptors can give us that — witness Dürer's Melancolia, Leonardo's Mona Lisa, Michelangelo's figures in the Chapel of the Medici. But these are not words. The infinite variety of pleasure and pain can no more be expressed directly by words than the endless play of light and color on the sea. Words do not love, hate, suffer, enjoy, any more than they taste, or smell, or are soft or cool; they have not in themselves passion, as they have not solidity or line. Yet, again, if I am a poet, they are my only medium. What is my way out? I must translate once more:

> O Spartan dog,
> More fell than anguish, hunger, or the sea!

> Surprised by joy, impatient as the wind.

> We watch'd her breathing thro' the night,
>   Her breathing soft and low,
> As in her breast the wave of life
>   Kept heaving to and fro.

Yet in these thoughts myself almost despising —
Haply I think on thee: and then my state,
Like to the lark at break of day arising
From sullen earth, sings hymns at Heaven's gate.

To put my feelings into words, no less than to record my impressions of sensuous things, I must relate them to something else.

The basic convention of imagery, then, has its roots in the essential limitations of the poet's medium; in the fact that language itself stands in no immediate relation to the objects which it represents, but is a congeries of conventional symbols — of symbols which themselves, as it happens, owe alike their origin and growth to innumerable similar transfers. For the substance of poetry is also the very stuff of words. And in its larger sense as well, the language of poetry is made up inevitably of symbols — of symbols for things in terms of other things, for things in terms of feelings, for feelings in terms of things. It is a language not of objects, but of the complex relations of objects. And the agency that moulds it is the ceaselessly active power that is special to poetry only in degree — *imagination*, that fuses the familiar and the strange, the thing I feel and the thing I see, the world within and the world without, into a *tertium quid* that interprets both. Open Shakespeare anywhere:

Thou are not conquer'd: beauty's ensign yet
Is crimson in thy lips and in thy cheeks,
And death's pale flag is not advanced there.

Pluck from the memory a rooted sorrow,
Raze out the written troubles of the brain.

Put out the light, and then put out the light.
If I quench thee, thou flaming minister,
I can again thy former light restore,
Should I repent me; but once put out thy light,
Thou cunning'st pattern of excelling nature,
I know not where is that Promethean heat,
That can thy light relume. When I have pluck'd
    the rose
I cannot give it vital growth again,
It needs must wither.

There are the two worlds — on the one hand, thought and affliction, passion, hell itself; on the other, what we have heard, what we have seen with our eyes, what we have looked upon, and our hands have handled — each incomplete without the other; each, in a true sense, non-existent without the other. And poetry mediates between the two; or rather, it brings the two together into one. And this is not rhapsody, but sober truth.

"Life, and Emotion, and I" — so Matthew Arnold once summed up the poet's triad. I should put it somewhat differently. There are two vivid sonnets of Sir Philip Sidney, the first and the fifteenth in "Astrophel and Stella," which deal with the exigencies of the poet's problem. Their endings will help me to what I mean:

> Thus, great with child to speak, and helpless
> in my throes;
> Biting my truant pen, beating myself for spite:
> "Fool!" said my Muse to me, "look in thy heart,
> and write!"

So the first. "But if," says the second,

> But if (both for your love and skill) your name
> You seek to nurse at fullest breasts of Fame;
> Stella behold! and then begin to endite.

"*Look in your heart* and *write*"; "*Stella behold* and *write*": there, in summary form, is the eternal triangle of the poet's art — what you feel, what you see, what you say: emotion, an object, and speech. And speech, like a shuttle, plays back and forth between the other two — the feeling and the thing — weaving a fabric from both, that is yet neither.

For we must come at once to a second fundamental attribute of poetry which follows from the first. I have tried to make clear how the convention of imagery grows out of the essential character of the poetic medium. But imagery, or rather the basic necessity that lies behind it, carries with it as a corollary a mass of conventions which we may sum up broadly as the World of Illusion. And that means — what?

Here we are at once on ticklish ground. I eagerly desire to steer clear of metaphysics, the perilous edge of which I am circumspectly skirting. For I am compelled to speak of appearance, and reality, and fact, and truth, and by instinct I shy at the terms. Let us, however, make the plunge, holding firmly to the concrete as a life line.

I have said that poetry builds up a fabric out of the relations of things different, yet alike. It does not deal with objects *per se*, but with objects as they appear to *us*. It must paint the thing as it sees it — not, alas! for the god of things as they are, who presumably sees them as they are, but for us mortals, who see them not at all as they are, but simply as they seem. And the poet's business is with appearances, not facts. That is a hard saying. Instead of dogmatizing, let us go to the fountain-head, to poetry itself. In 1833 Tennyson wrote, in "The Miller's Daughter":

> Remember you that pleasant day
>   When, after roaming in the woods,
> ('T was April then), I came and lay
>   Beneath those *gummy* chestnut buds
> That glistened in the April blue.

The *Quarterly* paid its respects with alacrity to the chestnut buds, and with some reason. Gummy they indubitably were, but what under Heaven had that incontrovertible fact of nature to do with what the lover saw? He was n't at the moment climbing trees in the Hesperides to finger fruit; he was looking at a shining object. And in 1842 the offending lines became:

> . . . I came and sat
> Below the chestnuts, when their buds
> Were glistening to the breezy blue.

That gives the truth of appearance; the truth of fact (to wit, stickiness) is at the moment sheer impertinence. Take a somewhat different case. In the "Ancient Mariner," as printed in the "Lyrical Ballads," occurred the familiar lines:

> The fair breeze blew, the white foam flew,
> The furrow *followed* free.

Later, in "Sibylline Leaves," the second line was printed thus:

> The furrow *stream'd off* free.

And Coleridge appended to the revised line a note:

In the former editions the line was, "The furrow followed free." But I had not been long on board a ship, before I perceived that this was the image as seen by

a spectator from the shore, or from another vessel.
From the ship itself the *Wake* appears like a brook
flowing off from the stern.

Perfectly true, and truth of appearance at that.
But supererogatory truth of fact lurks behind
the change, none the less. For the Mariner, as
Coleridge's intellect, hunting alone, perceived,
was on the ship, not off it, and so should see the
furrow streaming away, not following. But to
obtrude that fact is to snap the spell — to take
the Ancient Mariner from the mystery of his
silent sea and set him, an old sailor, at the stern
of a boat. A line that is as inevitable as the near-
ing of the spectre-bark itself was marred by a
meticulous observance of irrelevant truth of fact.
And eleven years later, with his unruly intellect
in its place again, Coleridge restored the original
reading.

It is unnecessary to labor the point. Poetry,
both the old and the newest of the new, is compact of what *seems*, not of what *is*; of what, if
taken literally, never was, on sea or land. Ponder
the following statements, regarded as matters
of fact:

> Lie still and deep,
> Sad soul, *until the sea-wave washes*
> *The rim o' the sun.*

All in the hot and copper sky,
The *bloody* Sun, at noon,
Right up above the mast did stand,
No bigger than the Moon.

Large and smoky red the sun's *cold disk* drops,
Clipped by naked hills, on violet shaded snow.

I wept as I remember'd how often you and I
Had tired the sun with talking and sent him down the sky.

Part of a moon was falling down the west,
Dragging the whole sky with it to the hills.

Like a four-sided wedge
The Custom House Tower
Pokes at the low, flat sky,
Pushing it farther and farther up.

Not one of these statements is literal fact; every
one of them is true, as a transcript of appearance.
And all of them, and ten thousand others, grow
out of the fundamental necessities of art, and
directly out of the initial situation that I have
tried to sketch.

For art deals in *illusion*. Literal accuracy, even
when possible, is art's undoing. A tree painted
with sedulous exactness as a tree, would never
give the tree at all; painted as Corot paints it,
or Rembrandt etches it, it's more a tree than if
it were a tree. The tension sensed behind the
thirty-one lines, that take less than two minutes

to repeat, between "'T is now struck twelve" and "the bell then beating one," in the first scene of "Hamlet," *is*, to all intents and purposes, an hour; sixty literal minutes of intervening talk on the stage would drag it to eternity. These are truisms. But it is the essence of art that its creations seem more true than if they were true — as Hamlet is truer than John Jones. Consider, for a moment, the titanic grandeur of Shakespeare's later heroes — that something colossal, like Michelangelo's figures, of which Professor Bradley speaks. Othello, Macbeth, Lear, Coriolanus, Anthony, are not transcripts of reality. They are truer than if they were. And it is because they can't be actual that they can be true — precisely as it is because Rembrandt's medium can't emulate a camera, that he can paint the Night Watch; precisely as a medium that can't present directly actual space becomes thereby capable of suggesting the depths beyond depths through which the eye is carried in some great landscapes. It is the fact that words are not and cannot be attached to things, that leaves them free, so that out of the very limitations of the medium comes liberty. And it is again no rhapsody, but sober, even scientific truth, to say that it is because Keats could not reproduce in words a window, that he could give us "magic casements,,opening on the foam Of perilous seas in faëry lands forlorn."* If the artistic medium, of whatever sort, were capable of actual reproduction, there would be no art. For the "effects of grandeur," to use a pregnant phrase of Meredith's, "are wrought out through a series of illusions, that are illusions to the sense within us only when divorced from the groundwork of the real." But it is that divorce which true art never makes.

For true illusion (if the paradox may be permitted), though it may be a dome in air, springs from the ground. It exists, because the law is ineluctable that the actual must be translated. But it is, on the other hand, the actual that rouses the poet's inner vision, and sets it assorting and weaving its thousand materials. Keats wrote to Reynolds from Winchester:

I never liked stubblefields so much as now — Aye better than the chilly green of the Spring. Somehow, a stubblefield looks warm — in the same way that some pictures look warm. This struck me so much in my Sunday's walk that I composed upon it.

There is reality — a stubblefield. There, too, is the bald statement of the impression of a stubblefield on Keats: "[I like] stubblefields better than the chilly green of Spring . . . somehow a

stubblefield looks warm." And here is the translation of the impression into art, in the "Ode to
Autumn":

> Who hath not seen thee oft amid thy store?
>   Sometimes whoever seeks abroad may find
> Thee sitting careless on a granary floor,
>   Thy hair soft-lifted by the winnowing wind;
> Or on a half-reap'd furrow sound asleep,
>   Drows'd with the fume of poppies, while thy hook
>   Spares the next swath and all its twinèd flowers:
> And sometimes like a gleaner thou dost keep
>   Steady thy laden head across a brook;
>   Or by a cider-press, with patient look,
>   Thou watchest the last oozings hours by hours.
>
> Where are the songs of Spring? Ay, where are they?
>   Think not of them, thou hast thy music too, —
> While barrèd clouds bloom the soft-dying day,
>   And touch the stubble-plains with rosy hue.

There are the stubblefields, and the spirit that
haunts them! Actual? No. True? Yes — if there
be any virtue and if there be any truth. Two days
earlier, after a delectable description of Winchester with its "excessively maiden-lady-like side
streets" and its "staid and serious knockers,"
Keats wrote to George and Georgiana Keats:

> Some time since I began a poem . . . quite in the
> spirit of town quietude. *I think I will give you the
> sensation of walking about an old country town in a coolish
> evening.*

And what he enclosed was the fragment of the

"Eve of St. Mark." Read it again, in the light of Keats's remark, and try your own hand at giving, in literal terms for actual things, "the spirit of town quietude"! And then ponder on the function of illusion. Poetry starts from the actual and ends in the true — as Coleridge started from the account of "the Citie Xandu," on the eightieth page of Purchas's Third Part, and ended in the vision of the stately pleasure-dome — shattered, alas! by the intrusion of another actuality in the guise of the "person on business from Porlock." Reality serves the artist, in Keats's own phrase, "as a starting-post towards all 'the two-and-thirty Palaces.'" For the poet is like Saul the son of Kish, who started out to find his father's asses — in a stubblefield, for aught I know — and found a kingdom.

Let me pause for a moment, to insist with the utmost explicitness that not one word that I have said runs counter to the demands of delicate and penetrating accuracy of observation, or of scrupulous fidelity to fact as it appears. Exactness of observation and illusion do not conflict. Some of the most significant recent verse, in particular, is compact of both. But that I wish to reserve for fuller discussion another time. Meanwhile let us proceed with our analysis.

The poet's truth which is presented through illusion is also truth tinged with *emotion*. There it differs fundamentally from that other aspect of truth which the scientist strives to catch and fix. And because the object of poetry, in the words of Wordsworth's famous pronouncement, is "truth . . . carried alive into the heart by passion," one element of poetic illusion is a heightening of actual fact. For emotion enhances reality, and truth of feeling, which is as veracious in its own sphere as truth of intellect, must be reckoned with as another object of the illusion of art. Take one brief line: "The desire of the moth for the *star*." The moth does not desire the star. The flame of the candle it may, and does, desire. But the magnificent and daring heightening in that one word has lifted the line from a statement of a fact of entomology into a poignant and unforgettable expression of one of the deepest truths of human life. "Poetry should surprise by a fine excess," wrote Keats, and that excess is at the heart of the illusion that exalts without deceiving.

> Tiger, Tiger, *burning bright*
> *In the forests of the night.*

There is not a shred of fact about that. Yet it is truth at white heat — the truth of terror and

mystery and baleful beauty, fused into one
flaming impression. And that is the very stuff
of poetry.

> Take, O take those lips away,
>   That so sweetly were forsworn;
> And those eyes, the break of day,
>   Lights that do mislead the morn!

> Thy soul was like a Star, and dwelt apart;
> Thou hadst a voice whose sound was like
>   the sea:
> Pure as the naked heavens, majestic, free,
> So didst thou travel on life's common way.

> My bounty is as boundless as the sea,
> My love as deep.

> And I will luve thee still, my dear,
>   Till a' the seas gang dry:
> Till a' the seas gang dry, my dear,
>   And the rocks melt wi' the sun.

Do we believe these things? In the answer to that
question we come from another angle back to the
heart of the matter.

For what we may call the language of poetry
in the larger sense — and that includes illusion
— exists under precisely the same conditions as
words themselves. And words mean what we
mean them to mean, and what we accept them
as meaning, and nothing else. It is concurrence
alone, not logic, that determines their signifi-

cance. If I say that blackberries are red when they are green, I mean what you take me to mean, not the kaleidoscopic sequence of contradiction that logic finds in my remark. Consent is the be-all and end-all of speech. Now illusion also means what it is meant to mean, and what we accept it as meaning. It's a glorified "Let's play," if you will, in the sense that, like children "pretending" (Stevenson's "Lantern Bearers," say), we see through it, and yet believe. Amiel was right when he spoke of "that poetical and artistic illusion *which does not aim at being confounded with reality itself*." It neither aims at it, nor do we understand it so, and to see that, is to clear our minds of endless confusion. John Dryden's robust common sense is at one with Amiel's critical acumen: "For a play," says he, "is still an imitation of nature; *we know we are to be deceived, and we desire to be so*." And we do not balk at the sea-wave washing the rim of the sun, which we know it does not do, any more than we boggle at blackberries that are red when they are green, although we know the colors as colors to be mutually exclusive. We simply exercise "*that willing suspension of disbelief for the moment*, which," as Coleridge says, "constitutes poetic faith." In a word, illusion is a convention

— a convention which poetry shares with the other arts. And its roots, on the one hand, are in the nature of the poetic medium itself, and on the other, in that common consent which underlies the possibility of all communication whatsoever.

Now, granted this presupposition (and it is axiomatic), it follows that the sole criterion of the truth of illusion is its inner congruity. Let me make that clear, first from some instances of the poets' striving to attain it, and then by a few examples of how it is broken in upon.

There is no more illuminating commentary on the art of poetry than the poets' own revision of their work. And that revision is constantly directed towards keeping the illusion true. I have already used a passage from "The Miller's Daughter" to point another moral. The first line of the stanza which immediately succeeds the one which immortalized the "gummy chestnut buds," begins as follows:

> A water-rat from off the bank
> Plunged in the stream.

Upon that, too, the *Quarterly* poured out the vials of its scorn, and once more with reason. Not, let me hasten to protest, because a water-rat is unpoetical. Mice and rats and such small deer are perfectly in place in poetry, when they *are* in place. They are triumphantly at home in "The Jolly Beggars," when

> . . . staggering, and swaggering,
> He roar'd this ditty up . . .
> While frighted rattons backward leuk
> And seek the benmost bore.

But the associations that cluster about rats clash as sharply with the other associations that Tennyson happens to be evoking in his picture, as those same associations accord with the magnificent Hogarthianism of "The Jolly Beggars." It is not of the slightest moment whether, in point of fact, a water-rat jumped, or an otter, or a turtle, or a frog. Tennyson is not rehearsing facts of natural history; he is striving for consistency of impression. And in 1842 the water-rat disappeared forever, and instead:

> *Then leapt a trout.* In lazy mood
> I watch'd the little circles die.

Let me be extremely explicit again: the point is not that a trout is more poetic than a water-rat. It is simply that the one destroys, the other helps create, the particular illusion that Tennyson at the moment was seeking to create.

That is a rather obvious example, from a poem where the creative energy was working (I think it must be said) at low tension. Take another, this time of the highest imaginative quality. Here are the first ten lines of "Hyperion," as they now stand.

> Deep in the shady sadness of a vale
> Far sunken from the healthy breath of morn,
> Far from the fiery noon, and eve's one star,
> Sat gray-hair'd Saturn, quiet as a stone,
> Still as the silence round about his lair;
> Forest on forest hung about his head
> Like cloud on cloud. No stir of air was there,
> Not so much life as on a summer's day
> Robs not one light seed from the feather'd grass,
> But where the dead leaf fell, there did it rest.

There, if it ever was secured, is absolute truth of illusion, and flawless consistency of the imagery that creates it: "eve's one star," "quiet as a stone," "still as the silence," "forest on forest" hanging motionless "like cloud on cloud" — the landscape and its one Titanic central figure permeated with utter stillness, remoteness, silence, majesty. But Keats wrote first — to take two lines only:

> Not so much life as a *young vulture's* wing
> Would spread upon a field of *green-ear'd* corn —

on second thought deleting the vulture in favor of an eagle. What has happened? A world that is motionless as death and hueless as despair, is broken in upon by a vulture's flight, and the vivid freshness of the summer's green. The whole key is changed. And so Keats cancelled the lines, and wrote in the margin of the manuscript:

> Not so much life as on a summer's day
> Robs not at all *the dandelion's* fleece.

But fleece or no fleece, the dandelion's blithe and sunny gold snaps utterly the spell. And at last, in the proof-sheets, the elusive harmony was captured once for all:

> Not so much life as on a summer's day
> Robs not one light seed from the feathered grass.

And the landscape is now motionless and hueless from hanging cloud to fallen leaf. It is the stuff that dreams are made on, to be sure, not fact. But it has the supreme truth of poetry, which is inviolate consistency with itself.

I resolutely resist the temptation to illustrate further, even though there beckons me Wordsworth's substitution of "the whistling rustic tending his plough" for "the rural milk-maid by her cow," in the Toussaint L'Ouverture sonnet, and a score of other alluring possibilities. For I want a moment for that other shattering of illusion which comes by way of the intrusion of fact. And since Wordsworth at his best is in-

fallible in his touch, and as unerring as a shaft of
light, we may take him without scruple at his
worst, if only to justify the airy charm he works
when he inherits Prospero's staff and book. Consider, accordingly, a stanza from "The Thorn."
Wordsworth tells us himself that the poem arose
out of his observing "on the ridge of Quantock
Hill, on a stormy day, a thorn which [he] had
often past, in calm and bright weather, without
noticing it." "I said to myself," he continues,
"'Cannot I by some invention do as much to
make this Thorn permanently an impressive
object as the storm has made it to my eyes at
this moment?' I began the poem accordingly."
That, you will observe, is very like Keats and
his stubblefield — except that Keats did not say
to himself: "Go to; let us make a stubblefield
impressive." At all events, no one ever set himself more doggedly than Wordsworth in this
instance, to create the fabric of illusion out of
the raw material of reality. I shall take but one
stanza:

> High on a mountain's highest ridge,
> Where oft the stormy winter gale
> Cuts like a scythe, while through the clouds
> It sweeps from vale to vale —

So far we are on the heights (even if not very

near the summit), fairly safe in the airy citadel
of poetry. But the stanza remorselessly proceeds:

> *Not five yards* from the mountain path,
> This Thorn you *on your left* espy;
> And to the left, *three yards beyond*,
> You see a little muddy pond
> *Of water* — never dry,
> Though but of compass small, and bare
> To thirsty suns and parching air.

The illusion is precipitated; the spell is snapt
again, "as the fractured point of a Prince
Rupert's tear reduces the crystal globule to
sand." For poetic truth and literal fact are like
the Franklin's love and lordship:

> Love wol nat ben constreyned by maistrye;
> Whan maistrie comth, the god of love anon
> Beteth his wings, and farewel! he is gon!

And poetic truth lies buried in the little muddy
pond with its meticulously ascertained dimensions:

> I've measured it from side to side,
> 'T is three feet long, and two feet wide.

"I do not know," says Audrey to Touchstone,
"what 'poetical' is. Is it honest in deed and
word? Is it a true thing?" "No, truly," says
Touchstone, *"for the truest poetry is the most
feigning."* Out of the mouth of fools comes forth
wisdom (when the voice is the voice of Shake-

speare!), but poetry in quest of fact has sometimes evinced a kinship with the bewildered
intellect of Audrey.

I am dwelling persistently upon illusion, because the fundamental conventions of poetry
grow inevitably out of the fact that art is what
it is, a translation, not a transcript, of reality.
And there is another question which it is necessary to ask about illusion. Are there other postu-
lates with which it dare not clash — that say to
illusion: "Thus far shalt thou go, and no farther?"
Two such checks and balances, I think, present
themselves.

In the first place, common sense does not
abdicate its throne. The willing suspension of
disbelief may not be strained too far. Even the
incredible is subject to standards of credibility.
Aristotle, who knew everything, knew that. Better a probable impossibility, he declares, than
an improbable possibility. We grant the world
of illusion freely, but once granted, we demand
that it shall have its own probability. For illusion
carries no license to play at ducks and drakes
with the materials which it combines. Dryden,
in his "Apology for Heroic Poetry and Poetic
License," quotes what he regards as the best
"example of excellent imaging" from his own

"State of Innocence and Fall of Man." Here it is:

> Seraph and cherub, careless of their charge,
> And wanton, in full ease now live at large;
> Unguarded leave the passes of the sky,
> *And all dissolved in hallelujahs lie.*

Then he proceeds: "I have heard (says one of [my well-natured censors]) of anchovies dissolved in sauce; but never of an angel in hallelujahs. A mighty witticism!" he continues, . . . "He might have burlesqued Virgil too, from whom I took the image: 'They invade the city, buried in sleep and wine.' A city's being buried, is just as proper on occasion, as an angel's being dissolved in ease, and songs of triumph." So Dryden, dragging a red herring across the trail with admirable dexterity. For "buried in sleep" or "dissolved in *ease*" unite two impressions which the usage of imagery permits to merge. But seraphs and cherubs dissolved in *hallelujahs* violate what Coleridge calls "the chosen laws controlling choice," of art. Shakespeare's instinct was infallible, when he substituted, in revising "Hamlet," "the *morn* in russet mantle clad" for "the *sun* in russet mantle clad," that "walks o'er the dew of yon high mountain top." The sun walking in a russet mantle remains untranslated, so to speak; the sun stays sun, and the mantle a mantle, as angels remain insoluble in hallelujahs. The morn in russet mantle, walking o'er the dew of yon high eastward hill is, on the other hand, a blending of images in entire accord with the tacit understanding that controls illusion. And observe: though we stickle at the sun clad in a russet mantle, we accept the perfect fusion of impressions in:

> Where the great Sun begins his state,
> *Robed in flames and amber light.*

The union there has to the full what Coleridge calls "credibilizing effect." It is just that effect which we miss, I think, in the case of Francis Thomson's poppy:

> With burnt mouth red like a lion's it drank
> The blood of the sun as he slaughter'd sank.

The poppy's "burnt mouth red like a lion's," and the "blood of the slaughtered sun," magnificently daring as they are, strain my poetic credulity to the breaking point. The illusion shattered because the translation of the actual is into terms themselves too potently actual to merge. The supreme transmutation into the very quintessence of truth in "Tiger, tiger, burning bright," is absent.

Have I made clear what I mean? Illusion is

not lawless. It is a world apart, if you please, but within it are its own necessities, which exact inexorable adherence to their mandates, if the world which we have willed is to exist at all. That is one check upon illusion. Is there another?

There are what we call the laws of nature. Dare the poet run counter to these? May he venture, for example, since he may represent the sun as old and feeble, or may speak of its cold disk — may he also represent it as *setting in the East?* He may *modify* actual fact; may he also *contradict* it? There has been a good deal of dust raised about the question, but, like the others, it reduces wholly, in the last analysis, to a matter of acceptance. How far do we stretch our willing suspension of disbelief that constitutes poetic faith? That is the sole criterion. Well, there is no question of our extending the suspension to include *transcendence* of natural law. We accept without an instant's hesitation, in the "Ancient Mariner," the spectre-bark, and all the supernatural agencies that underlie the action of the poem. Like ghosts and fairies and spells, those belong to the misty midregion of our racial as well as literary inheritance, towards which we cherish at least the poetical will to believe. We do not, on the other hand, unless I am mistaken, accept *violation* of natural law — if we know it. If, in the "Ancient Mariner," we think that the "one bright star *within the nether tip*" of the moon means what Coleridge pretty certainly did n't mean it to mean, — namely, that the Mariner saw a star through the solid, opaque body of the moon, — we balk, and begin to write notes upon the error. For that is n't part of the spell that we accept; it contradicts universal experience, and does violence to that stubborn persuasion within us which Dr. Johnson felt, when he refuted Bishop Berkley by "striking his foot with mighty force against a stone." In a word, a star seen through the moon is in a wholly different category from a spectre-bark. The last we freely acquiesce in; if we understand the first to be *meant*, our suspension of disbelief terminates forthwith.

I said, a moment ago, that we do not accept violation of natural law, *if we know it*. The poet may, on the other hand, make such things be, and overcome us like a summer's cloud, without our special wonder. But if he does it successfully, he must seem not to have done it. And that way peril lies. For in this particular quarter of the world of appearance there holds good, I fear, the sad truth that applies to sin: "man may securely sin, but safely never" — or at least, hardly ever. Still, in seeming as in sin, it is sometimes done, and here is a case in point.

On the evening of April 18, 1827, Goethe laid before Eckermann an engraving of a landscape of Rubens, and asked him to point out what he saw. Eckermann named the outstanding details of the picture.

"Good," said Goethe, "that would seem to be all. But you've missed the main point. All these objects that we see before us there — the herd of sheep, the hay-cart, the horses, the reapers going home — from which side are they lighted?" "They have the light," said I, "on the side turned towards us, and throw the shadows into the picture. Particularly, the reapers in the foreground are in strong light, which produces a fine effect." "Through what, however, has Rubens brought about this beautiful effect?" "Through the fact," I replied, "that he throws these bright figures against a dark background." "But this dark background," persisted Goethe, "how does it come to be there?" "It is the strong shadow," said I, "that the clump of trees throws towards the figures." "But how is that?" I continued, in astonishment. "The figures throw their shadow *into* the picture, the clump of trees, on the other hand, throws its shadow *towards the spectator!* So we have the light from two opposite sides; but that's really contrary to all nature."

Now may I interrupt the conversation at this point to observe that the invaluable Eckermann did n't *see* the violation of nature until Goethe had performed the Socratic function with truly national efficiency. And what is more, we may be reasonably certain that Rubens did n't *mean* the Eckermanns to see it. The Goethes he'd have to reckon with. To resume:

"That's just the point," replied Goethe, with a little smile. "It's through this that Rubens shows himself a master, and proclaims that he stands with free spirit above nature, and treats it in accordance with his higher ends. The double light is certainly audacious, and you can always say that it's contrary to nature. But if it is contrary to nature, then I say along with that, that it is higher than nature; I say that it is the daring touch of the master, through which he makes clear, as genius can, that art is not wholly subject to physical necessity, but has its own laws."

And now observe the distinction that is made:

"The artist," continued Goethe, "must undoubtedly follow nature in details with scrupulous piety; he may not arbitrarily alter the conformation of the skeleton or the position of muscles and sinews in an animal, so that thereby its individual character is infringed upon. For that would be to nullify nature. But in the higher regions of artistic technique whereby a picture becomes a real picture, he has freer play, and here he may proceed even to such arbitrary devices as Rubens has used, in the double light."

In a word, we are back at appearance again. If there is in a work of art a contravention of nature, and the resulting effect seems more true than if it were true, the artist, be he painter or poet, is justified when he speaketh, and we clear when we judge. There are infringements upon natural law which we flatly refuse, under any circumstances, to accept. There are others where the artist, put to his shifts, has a fighting chance to win our assent. But at best artistic illusion runs counter to the laws of nature at its peril. There are always commentators in the background making notes, and then Eckermann is as wise as Goethe.

We have been discussing appearance and reality in poetry, with our eye, for the most part, on the physical world. But that is only half of the content of poetry. "I would to heaven," scrawled Byron, on the back of the manuscript of "Don Juan" —

> I would to heaven that I were so much clay,
> As I am blood, bone, marrow, passion, feeling.

There, in "blood, bone, marrow, passion, feeling," is the other reality. Can the poet give us that directly, or must he there again translate? We have already looked at the question from one angle. I wish now, very briefly, to bring it into connection with what has just been said about illusion.

Consider, for a moment, the poet in relation to

his audience: on the one hand, feeling at its keenest edge and highest tension; on the other the
low, placid, unruffled level of our normal moods.
"The faint conceptions I have of poems to
come," wrote Keats, "bring the blood frequently
into my forehead." Our blood courses quietly in
our veins. Does the poet — can he indeed — convey to us, cool, collected, serene, the intense
emotion which he feels? Does he even himself go
on feeling at white heat? Or must there once
more be a transfer of some sort?

Let us put the matter briefly to the test. Recall
the great elegies in English. Do they, on the one
hand, express the poignancy of grief? Do they,
on the other, stir grief in us who read them? I
name, for instance, "Astrophel," "Lycidas,"
"Adonais," "Thyrsis." And the very titles are
at once significant — not Philip Sidney, but
Astrophel; not Edward King, but Lycidas; not
John Keats, but Adonais; not Arthur Hugh
Clough, but Thyrsis. And all four poems are
either steeped in pastoral imagery, or similarly
set off from actuality. But for the moment the
one question which I wish to ask is this: Does
any one feel grief on reading any of these elegies?
Did the poets themselves, as they wrote them?
I shall leave my questions, which are not rhetori-

cal, unanswered for a moment. For, you will say, they are none of them, these four great elegies, the expressions of deep personal loss. There was never more than sadness. That may well be. Let us grant it without discussion, and take another group of four, in which the underlying personal grief was certainly present. Tennyson's "In Memoriam" grows out of the loss of a close and dear friend — a loss which darkened the poet's life for years. Emerson's "Threnody" springs from the loss of an only son; Meredith's "A Faith on Trial," from the death of the poet's wife; Whitman's "When Lilacs Last in the Dooryard Bloom'd," from the tragic taking off of a beloved leader. But in these, too, the bitterness of death is past, the poignancy of emotion has softened into recollection. The poet is no longer merely the friend, the father, — compare with Emerson's "Threnody" the exceeding bitter cry: "O my son Absalom, my son, my son Absalom! would God I had died for thee, O Absalom, my son, my son!" — he is no longer the husband, the lover of a dead leader, but the *artist*. The grief has not ceased to be personal; it is still that. To believe otherwise would be to impugn a great sincerity. But what has happened? The poet is no longer swept from his moorings, no longer, like Ugolino, turned to stone within; he is, in a true sense, outside his grief — *as we are*. And because he is an artist, his grief has become to him as living clay for the potter's wheel. It must take form. And it can take form only when it is looked back upon, or down upon, or through. And what we feel is not grief at all, but a lofty tranquillity, a deep beauty, wrung from grief, but no longer grief itself.

There has, then, been a translation — the most momentous which poetry can make: the transmutation of its ingredients into *beauty*. "Aus meinen grossen Schmerzen mach' ich die kleinen Lieder" — but the sorrows are not the songs. Grief, love, hate, at their height are "outrageous as a sea, dark, wasteful, wild." But the end of art, whose essence is restraint, is not to make us grieve, or love, or hate, or flush with anger, or grow pale with rage. It is to stir us with the sense of an imperishable beauty. And that sense is communicated only when the poet has been first submerged and then detached, when he has passed out of the very torrent, tempest, and whirlwind of passion — when "emotion *recollected in tranquillity*" has touched the springs of the imagination.

For the poet's feelings, like his stubblefield,

are only a starting-post to something which has
not their sort of reality at all.

> Ah, what avails the sceptered race!
>   Ah, what the form divine!
> What every virtue, every grace!
>   Rose Aylmer, all were thine.
>
> Rose Aylmer, whom these wakeful eyes
>   May weep, but never see,
> A night of memories and sighs
>   I consecrate to thee.

Emotion, formless, chaotic, fluid in itself, has
attained permanence, beauty, form. And in so
doing it has become something which it is not.

I have really been discussing, under the guise
of illusion, the nature of poetic truth. For the
very essence of poetic truth is accepted illusion.
That illusion, in turn, as we have also seen, grows
inevitably out of the limitations of the poet's
medium. And illusion to which we consent, with
all that that implies, is the taproot of the conventions of poetry. I wish now to turn, with the
utmost brevity, to one of the major conventions
which I shall discuss more fully in another chapter namely, rhythm.

The one and only thing I wish to say about
poetic rhythm now is this: It serves notice that
we are on the frontiers of illusion — "Enter

these enchanted woods, ye who dare!" That is, *the expectation with which we approach poetry* is utterly different from the expectation with which we approach prose. We stand ready to accept in the one what we reject, if we find it, in the other. And verse, whether directed to the ear or to the eye, is the outward and visible sign that we are entering the world where truth of literal fact yields place to another truth. It is the signal for that willing suspension of disbelief on which I have rung the changes. Consider a precisely parallel situation. What happens when we enter a theatre? We assume, more or less unconsciously, a definite attitude of mind towards what we know we are to see and hear: namely, time that is not real time; the heightening of make-up; tricks of light; asides and stage whispers that everybody hears; letters read aloud that no one ever reads aloud; it may be, long soliloquies; it may be, men and women speaking in blank verse. None of these things would we accept outside those walls. There, we know that what we are to be given is illusion, and we expect and we desire to undergo it. That is what we go for. Now the sight or sound of verse stands to poetry in precisely the relation in which the rising of the curtain stands to the play. When we hear verse or see it, we pass

from one world to another, and we expect to pass.
We shall come back to this again, for it is fundamental in more ways than one. For the moment,
I have said enough when I repeat that verse,
metre, poetic rhythm or cadence (name it by
what name you will) serves notice that we are on
enchanted ground, and opens the door to the
illusion that is poetic truth — a city built to
music, therefore never built at all, and therefore
built forever.

Such, then, as I understand it, is the essential
nature of poetry — a fabric of truth based on
reality, but not reproducing reality. And the
constituent elements of the fabric have their
sanction in consent. Poetry is, in essence, of
convention all compact.

II

THE WAYS OF CONVENTIONS

CONVENTIONS exist by virtue of usage, and usage is, of all things human, the most capricious. The clothes I should wear were I speaking at eight instead of five are consecrated by usage to the hours whose appurtenance is fashion and ceremony — provided that those hours fall after sunset. What, it is pertinent to ask, would happen, were one to give a morning lecture garbed in evening clothes? Yet there is obviously neither rhyme nor reason in the requirement that I shall wear a certain coat only between certain stipulated hours, on pain of feeling the weight of the imponderables that rule the world. But that is usage — precisely as it is linguistic usage that permits imponderables to have weight — and usage is the source and origin of conventions. Now convention in poetry (as has been well said) is only the costume in which emotion attires itself, and it comes, like clothes, under the same capricious sway.

It is the behavior of conventions, then, with which we have now to do. There are, as we

have seen, certain fundamental conventions inherent in the very nature of poetry itself. But
all conventions are not so firmly rooted. Once
started on their way, they multiply and ramify
and split and merge, and it is the bewildering
and phantasmagoric variety of the branches
rather than their ultimate derivation from a
common root that I wish, if I can, to exhibit.

With the birth of the individual conventions
I shall not particularly concern myself. In one
sense conventions are not born at all. For whatever their ancestry, they never come into being
as conventions. It is only when they are taken up
through acceptance into usage that they acquire
conventionality. "The heroic couplet," says
Professor Manly, with the utmost truth, "origi-
nated . . . suddenly. Chaucer wrote heroic couplets, and there they were." But when Chaucer
wrote heroic couplets, and there all at once they
were, the heroic couplet did not thereby spring
into existence as a convention. It became that
later, when other poets, following Chaucer,
looked upon it and saw that it was good, and
wore it threadbare.

Yet it is sometimes possible to see how this,
that, and the other convention began. Conventions frequently take their rise, for instance,

from the faulty essays of an early and as yet un-
developed technique. Dramatic conventions by
the dozen had some such origin. The germs of the
stage whisper and the aside and the soliloquy are
present in the naïve endeavors of a primitive
dramatic technique to produce its special illusion. After Noah has presented himself to the
audience, in the Hegge Miracle Plays —

> Noe, seres, my name is knowe;
> My wyff and my chyldere here on rowe —

his wife proceeds with the further enlightenment
of the spectators by giving to Noah presumably superfluous information:

> *I am your wyff, your childeryn these be.*

There is the artless device by which the early
drama strove to solve the technical problem of
imparting certain necessary facts to the audience
through a supposedly natural conversation between the *dramatis personæ*. And the footman
and parlor-maid of modern comedy represent
but a later stage in the evolution of the same
convention.

The essential point, however, is that conventions become conventions through wholesale
imitation, conscious or unconscious, of forms,
devices, methods of expression, which may them-

selves have had their origin in any of a hundred ways. There is nothing mysterious about the process. One does in letters, as in life, what one sees others doing. If anybody who has read for years the Contributors' Club of the *Atlantic* aspires to become a contributor himself, he falls, half consciously, half instinctively, into the prevailing tone (if he can) of that delightful *causerie* — a prevailing tone which it has, please mark, because hundreds of other contributors have been doing just that thing. If, on the other hand, he addresses his observations to the New York *Nation* he finds himself, more or less unconsciously, curbing and pruning his style to fit the *Nation's* more austere conventions. And all this may not mean in the least that one is merely, even consciously at all, perhaps, "playing the sedulous ape." One simply follows the path of least resistance. And very much so, not in any specially occult or thaumaturgic way, one has to think of literary conventions as arising. The innate human tendency to imitation, coupled with that other formidable phenomenon which we call habit, does the business.

Out of the seeming chaos, however, of poetic conventions emerge two weighty and paradoxical facts, which have influenced the development of poetry from its beginnings, and are potent still to-day: the plasticity of conventions, while the life still runs in their veins; and their tendency (if I may change the figure) to harden into empty shells, like abandoned chrysalids when the informing life has flown. And through these two opposing characteristics of convention, it comes about that art moves from stage to stage by two divergent paths: on the one hand, by moulding the still ductile forms; on the other, by shattering the empty shells — the way of constructive acceptance, and the way of revolt. Each has its place, because each grows out of the ways of conventions themselves. What I have to say now, accordingly, looks directly forward to the underlying theme of the remainder of our discussion.

We shall be clear only by being very concrete. And I am going this time to draw my illustrations chiefly from mediæval poetry, and more especially from Chaucer. Nor shall I make any secret of my reasons. One is the fact that the older conventions, through their very unfamiliarity, stand out to us in sharp detachment as conventions. They are not, as in the case of contemporary poetry, part and parcel of what for most of us is a subtle texture of personal associations and predilections. And since I am anxious to isolate and disengage the conventions as conventions, the freedom from disturbing modern implications is, for the moment, valuable. Moreover, quite frankly, I am doing what I do just now, because the Middle Ages are so tremendously alive. For while they lasted, please perpend, they were not the Middle Ages at all. They had n't the faintest idea that they were mediæval; to themselves they were as "modern" as we think we are. And they were as blissfully ignorant of what we in our wisdom were going to think of them and tag them, as we are mercifully oblivious of what succeeding centuries are going to think of (and label) us. For we too shall be — Heaven only knows what, but most certainly not "modern," soon enough. "Stop! careless youth," the fourteenth century might cry from its crypts to our self-styled modernity:

> Stop! careless youth, as you pass by;
> As you are now, so once was I;
> As I am now, so you will be.

"*As you are now, so once was I*" — that homely "Hark from the tombs," then, I should like to propose, for the moment, not as a *memento mori*, but as a *vade mecum*. For the poet of the Middle Ages was in essentials altogether such an one as ourselves.

I have said, then, for one thing, that conventions are plastic, so long as they are alive. Let us consider, to begin with, their capability of forming new attachments. And I know no more illuminating instance of this particular trick than the case of the rose and the daisy in Chaucer's century.

In the first place, the rose and the lady of the lover's dream were identified. That is the theme of the most remarkable and influential of all the mediæval allegories, the "Roman de la Rose." And as time went on, the perfections of the flower were carried over bodily to the lady. We are familiar with the transfer yet: "Oh, my Luve's like a red, red rose"; "Queen rose of the rosebud garden of girls" — and all the rest. The convention as such has its roots in the tendency that has already been discussed at length. But now a new and most interesting factor enters into the life of this particular poetic commonplace. Through the celebration by a group of French courtly poets of the charms of certain ladies whose name was Marguerite, the *daisy* became the fashionable symbol for the poet's mistress. What happened? The wealth of conventions that had gathered about the rose was transferred, through the accident of a lady's name, *in toto* to the *marguerite*.

And that carried with it a rather astonishing result. The marguerite falls heir to the possessions of the rose; the rose is endowed with fragrance; *ergo*, the daisy, which now represents the lady, must possess it too. And so it follows that the *marguerite*, in Machaut,

> Par excellence est garnie d'odour.

The poet, preternaturally acute, even smells the daisy from afar:

> Sa douce odeur qui de loing m'est présente.

And Froissart goes so far as to tell us where it got its fragrance:

> Zepherus li donna odours.

Deschamps more cautiously admits the possibility:

> Voir de tel fleur a maint l'odeur proufitte —

but he enters mild protest in another poem: "It is n't a flower that's puffed up, for its odor is n't haughty or fierce (car s'odeur n'est orgueilleuse ne fière)"! But it is Chaucer who caps the climax.

In the Prologue to the "Legend of Good Women," after the exquisite passage in which he describes his homage to "these floures whyte and rede, Swiche as men callen daysies in our toun," and pictures himself as

> Kneling alwey, til hit unclosed was,
> Upon the smale softe swote gras,

he goes on to tell how the grass was

> . . . with floures swote enbrouded al,
> Of swich swetnesse and *swich odour* over-al,
> That, for to speke of gomme, or herbe, or tree,
> Comparisoun may noon y-maked be;
> *For hit surmounteth pleynly alle odoures*,
> And eek of riche beautee alle floures.

The reference is plainly to the daisy, and the daisy — the English flower that Chaucer knew — is *odorless*. One recalls the well-known song that opens the "Two Noble Kinsmen," which happens to use odor as the distinguishing quality of the flowers it names:

> Roses, their sharp spines being gone,
> Not royal in their smells alone,
>   But in their hue;
> Maiden pinks, of odour faint,
> *Daisies smell-less*, yet most quaint,
>   And sweet thyme true.

Or, if one hesitates to trust the testimony of one poet against another, or even the evidence of one's proper nose, one may find impartial and scientific authority on the point from the herbalists of the sixteenth century down to the botanists of the twentieth. The English daisy has no odor, and never had. Chaucer speaks of its odor as beyond comparison with that of gum, or herb, or tree — as flatly surpassing all odors. "Whom," in Mr. Browning's impassioned words, "whom shall my soul believe?"

Well, the thing that had happened is obvious enough. The *marguerite*, like the rose, was but the symbol of the lady; the lady must be perfect and entire, wanting nothing in all the qualities inherent in a lady; therefore, her flower must be possessed of all the perfections of a flower. Fragrance is such a perfection; therefore it follows inevitably that the daisy must possess the attribute, for very much the same reason that to Anselm existence had to be predicated of the Deity. The fragrance of the rose was transferred to the daisy without a qualm. It had to have it, and realism looked the other way.

It continued, indeed, to keep its eyes averted. For I wish to ask you to observe another significant fact. For over five centuries not a soul but the much-maligned Godwin seems ever to have observed that Chaucer does represent the daisy as endowed with fragrance. The passage has been quoted times without number for what it is — one of the most charming descriptions of the flower in the whole range of English poetry. Most of us think of it, when we think of Chaucer, before any other lines except the Prologue to the

"Canterbury Tales." As Longfellow reads Chaucer, "from every page Rise odors of ploughed field" — incidentally, there is n't a ploughed field, except in one simile, in Chaucer — "or flowery mede." It's Eckermann and the Rubens landscape over again. The illusion is so complete that five centuries of English Eckermanns failed to observe that it was illusion, and not fact. Chaucer, in other words, has so vivified the convention that it seems truer than a transcript from reality.

Just that performance we should not, I presume, repeat to-day. Keats puts odorous daisies where, to our mind, they properly belong — namely, in the Elysian fields. There the bards of passion and of mirth are

> Seated on Elysian lawns
> Browsed by none but Dian's fawns;
> Underneath large blue-bells tented,
> *Where the daisies are rose-scented,*
> And the rose herself has got
> Perfume which on earth is not.

At the same time I am not at all sure that a daisy has n't as good a right to smell as a trumpet-flower to "bray and blare," which it does (with modesty enough and likelihood to lead it) in the most impeccably correct "new" poetry.

The transfer of qualities, then, from the rose

to the daisy is full of a number of things that il-
luminate the behavior of conventions. And similar shifts meet us on every hand. Since we have
been dealing with one odor which on earth is not,
let us give a moment to another.

The mediæval lover, particularly if he were
French or North Italian, was not unlikely, in his
panegyric of his lady, to identify her with a
panther. It was a commonplace of compliment.
And it arose through a perfectly normal transfer
of conventions. In the first place, the Middle
Ages found in Pliny's "Natural History" and a
treatise known as "Physiologus," a mine of useful and misleading information. The two together
furnished most of the data for the "unnatural
natural history" that ran riot as late as Lyly's
"Euphues." But the Middle Ages had their own
way of dealing with their facts. From still earlier
centuries had come down an inordinate fondness
for allegorizing everything on which allegory
could lay its hands. And so there sprang up
the Bestiaries, amazing compilations of beasts,
and birds, and fishes, endowed with qualities
they never had, and allegorized into types of
sacred things. And in the Bestiaries the panther holds an honorable place. Now the "fact"
about the panther was that it possessed a breath

of marvellous sweetness (a quality which it had in common with the whale), and this fragrant breath attracted other animals to it. So much for the fact. Allegorized, the panther became the type of Christ. For his sweetness draws all men to him. But so does the lady's sweetness draw her lovers. Accordingly, on the basis of a common quality transferred from one to the other, the panther became the symbol of the lady. That the panther's breath was not sweet, has nothing to do with the case. It was accepted as such, and that was enough. Nor does it matter in the least that the precisely similar endowment of the whale turned it into a symbol of the devil, who also exercises attraction. It is all as irrational as words or dress. For conventions *are* irrational. Yet let us be chary of casting the first stone. When the poet even now invokes his mistress as his dove, his star, his rose, his lily, he is performing a legerdemain with his conventions that is identically the same. We still acquiesce in the dove's gentleness, the lily's purity, the rose's beauty; we withhold acceptance from a panther breathing odors of Araby the Blest — and that is all. The conventions are different; their behavior is the same.

What we are concerned with for the moment,

please remember, is the freedom with which conventions form new attachments — a freedom which renders them susceptible of constantly new and varied use. Let us consider, now, a particularly interesting group of conventions which occur in one of the most finished masterpieces of subtly penetrating characterization in English poetry — the description of the Prioress in the Prologue to the "Canterbury Tales." It is a delicately ironical, yet exquisitely sympathetic portrayal of a clash of ideals. The Prioress is a nun; she is also very much a woman; and what Chaucer is depicting is the engagingly imperfect submergence of the feminine in the ecclesiastical. And he does it by a daring yet consummately adroit transference of conventions. At his disposal, on the one hand, was the mass of conventional phraseology indelibly stamped through long usage with the associations of the poetry of love; on the other hand, luminously present in his mind, and pervaded with his inalienable humor, was his conception of the devout and gentle Prioress, who has not only immortal but very mortal longings in her. And he achieves the impression which permeates the whole description — the impression of the hovering of the worthy lady's spirit between two worlds — by deftly carrying over to the nun conventions steeped in reminiscences of earthly love. It is the clash of associations between the two sets of conventions that creates the character. All this is generalizing; let us come to the thing itself.

There were two words with which every reader of French poetry in Chaucer's day (and everybody in Chaucer's circle read French poetry) had clearly defined and inevitable associations — "simple" and "coy." For "simple" alone, and "coy" alone, and "simple and coy" together, belong to the stock phraseology of fourteenth-century courtly poetry. The lady's eyes were simple (even Medea's among others) — usually simple as a dove; so was her look, her face, her voice, her speech, her smile, her bearing, and herself. "Coy" (which meant "quiet," with a touch sometimes of the demure, though not of coquetry) was applied by the lover to his mistress incessantly. And the combination of simple and coy (*simple et coie*) was no less a commonplace of the "sweet jargoning" of mediæval lovers. One of its favorite habitats was the *pastourelle*, and the engagingly frank and often frail young persons who are the heroines of the *genre* are uncommonly likely to be simple and coy. Nor is it less a pet locution of the inexorably

long-drawn catalogues of the lady's physical
charms. In a word, the phrase, so far as I know,
was confined to the poetry of courtly love, and
any lover to any lady was pretty certain to employ it. Now Chaucer begins his sketch of the
Prioress as follows:

> Ther was also a Nonne, a Prioresse,
> That of hir smyling was ful simple and coy.

There, in the second line, is struck the keynote of
the description. The convention did n't belong
to the nun at all, as nun. To every one of Chaucer's readers its distinctly earthly rather than
heavenly flavor was unmistakable. The first hint
of the clash between the woman and the nun is
dexterously given by the impinging, so to speak,
of two opposing auras of associations.

I must pass over the exquisite incongruity of
the nun's self-chosen, unecclesiastical, flower-
like name, Madame Eglantine, and her choice of
a one-time artist, and courtier, and lover of
beautiful attire, the French Saint Eloi, as her
favorite saint. For Chaucer is by no means done
with his shifting of old conventions to new uses.
And the next transfer is an audacious one. Start-
ing centuries before Chaucer with that ¡Bible
of mediæval chivalric practice, Ovid's "Art of

Love," and handed down through scores of poets
after him, there developed a code of conventional injunctions to lovers and ladies alike —
injunctions ranging from the fit of the lover's
clothes, and the care of his or her teeth and nails,
to the most esoteric doctrines of love's joys and
perils. High among these precepts stood observance of dainty manners (mediævally dainty, that
is to say) at table. And in a famous, even
notorious passage in Jean de Meun's part of the
"Roman de la Rose" the convention attains a
peculiarly vivid embodiment. For there an old
harridan, La Vielle, rehearses to a youth to
whom she has taken a liking, the checkered story
of her life, and descants at large, with intimate
detail, upon the failings of her sex. Among these
foibles are the wiles a woman uses to allure a
potential yet still demurring lover, and among
these, in turn, is her delicate behavior at the
table. Now come back to Geoffrey Chaucer and
his Prioress. What does he do next? He coolly
appropriates the lines from the "Roman de la
Rose"—lines which everybody knew as we know
Hamlet's soliloquy — and transfers them to
Madame Eglantine:

> At mete wel y-taught was she with-alle;
> She leet no morsel from hir lippes falle,

Ne wette hir fingres in hir sauce depe.
Wel coude she carie a morsel, and wel kepe,
That no drope ne fille up-on hir brest.
In curteisye was set ful muche hir lest.
Hir over lippe wyped she so clene,
That in hir coppe was no ferthing sene
Of grece, whan she dronken hadde hir draughte.
Ful semely after hir mete she raughte.

The smile of the Spirit of Comedy lurks behind the lines! And to every one of Chaucer's readers came the flash of delighted association from the rehearsal of the Prioress's dainty manners to the intent, distinctly more mundane than pious, of precisely these same manners as enjoined with gusto by the Duenna in the "Roman de la Rose."

But Chaucer is not yet done. The Prioress's dress and bearing, and her little dogs, and her tenderness of heart, must be passed over. We have still to be told how she looked. And that brings us to another of the amazing conventions of mediæval love poetry. For it was accepted poetic good form that the lover, writing of his lady, should inventory her charms from top to toe in good set terms, and with an anatomical exhaustiveness that extenuated nothing. There is the right and meet phrase for every feature; they occur with desolating unanimity in the pages of

a hundred poets. Her eyes must be gray or *vair* —
gray as a falcon, gray as a goose, gray as glass;
her mouth must be *petite, vermeille, riant;* her
nose *traitis* (a mediæval lady with an ill-propor-
tioned nose was rarer than the "soleyn fenix of
Arabye," of whom there was just one); her forehead broad, and high, and white, and polished
like ivory; her chin a little cleft; her face mingled
lily and rose. Read one, and you have all. Now
Chaucer describes the Prioress in five lines, but
every detail might have come from any fourteenth-century lover's description of his mistress:

> Hir nose tretys; hir eyen greye as glas;
> Hir mouth ful smal, and ther-to softe and reed;
> But sikerly she hadde a fair forheed;
> It was almost a spanne brood, I trowe;
> For, hardily, she was nat undergrowe.

The convention has been lifted bodily from its
attachment to the earthly lady and transferred,
with all its blushing associations thick upon it,
to the nun. Yet no less noteworthy than the skill
with which the lines suggest still youthful flesh
and blood behind the well pinched wimple, is the
restraint which foregoes the remainder of the
inevitable inventory, and leaves the Prioress
charmingly human, without a suggestion of the
sensuous.

Yet one more transfer and Chaucer is done. The closing lines of the sketch are these:

> Ful fetis was hir cloke, as I was war.
> Of smal coral aboute hir arm she bar
> A peire of bedes, gauded al with grene;
> And ther-on heng a broche of gold ful shene,
> On which ther was first write a crowned A,
> And after, *Amor vincit omnia.*

That is the most consummate touch of all. For the motto on the Prioress's brooch was a convention with a history. The line ("love conquers all things") is, as everybody knows, from one of Virgil's Eclogues. There it refers, of course, to the way of a man with a maid. But by a pious transfer, which took place long before Chaucer, and had behind it the strange jumble of mediæval superstitions about Virgil, the line was converted to the use of love celestial. Now is it earthly love that conquers all, now heavenly; the phrase plays back and forth between the two. And it is precisely that happy ambiguity of the convention — itself the result of an earlier transfer — that makes Chaucer's use of it here, as a final summarizing touch, a master stroke. *Which of the two loves does "amor" mean to the Prioress?* I do not know; but I think she thought she meant love celestial.

Throughout the masterly characterization, then, the hovering of the conventions between their two environments is the medium which Chaucer uses, with unerring skill, to convey the wavering of the Prioress's spirit between her two worlds.

I have dwelt on Chaucer's delineation of the Prioress, because it makes clear one of the two points I wish especially to emphasize. Conventions are not static. They form new attachments, acquire fresh content. And so far forth they are plastic stuff for the artist's hand.

But there is another important *modus operandi* of conventions. Not only do the same conventions acquire new content, but the same content may also assume new conventions. In other words, not only may outworn conventions achieve new life by forming fresh attachments, but outworn themes may be rejuvenated by taking on contemporary garb. This last procedure is one that never ceases. But again let us use, to begin with, a mediæval instance — the remarkable series of transformations, namely, that took place when the classical epic passed into the twelfth- and thirteenth-century romance. And in this case we can follow the successive metamorphoses straight down to our own time.

The Middle Ages seized on the great stories of
the classics with avidity. Their core of narrative
was felt as vividly alive; its sheath of epic machinery and classical mythology and obsolete
manners and customs, on the other hand, was
alien and remote. And so, when the "Æneid"
becomes the "Roman d'Eneas," and the "The-
baid" the "Roman de Thèbes," and the "Pharsalia" the "Roman de Julius César," and the
Homeric stories the "Roman de Troie," the narrative core persists, but the sheath of epic conventions has for the most part been sloughed off.
And in its place has developed a new and highly
significant integument, conventional to the last
degree, but now no longer classically, but mediævally conventional. The Middle Ages, that is
to say, translated the classical conventions into
terms of the commonplaces dear to their own
heart.

For one thing, the stage was completely reset,
and the actors recostumed. The classical heroes
and heroines were transmogrified into mediæval
knights and ladies; battles were turned into
tournaments; Greece, Rome, Troy, and Carthage
became twelfth- or thirteenth-century France.
We have already seen the mediæval ideal of
feminine beauty. And here, for instance, is what

Philomela becomes in the little romance that
Chrétien de Troyes made out of Ovid's sixth
Metamorphosis:

Forehead white and broad without wrinkle; eyes
clearer than jacinth, wide apart; straight eyebrows,
neither painted nor adorned; nose high, and long, and
straight; face with fresh color of roses and *fleur de lis;*
smiling mouth, lips full and a little redder than red
samite in grain; breath that smells sweeter than piment,
or balsam, or incense; little teeth, white, in a row; chin
and neck, throat and breast, whiter than any ermine —

and so on through two mortal pages more. And
Helen and Hecuba, Andromache, and Cassandra,
and Polyxena in the "Roman de Troie," Dido
and Lavinia in the "Eneas," Antigone and Ismene in the "Thèbes," and Cleopatra in the
"Roman de Julius César" agree in foreheads,
noses, eyes, and chins with each other and with
all the ladies of the poets of the day, precisely as
in the eighteenth-century gardens "grove answers grove, And every alley has its brother."
Greek and Roman and Trojan heroes joust in
accordance with the canons of chivalry, garbed
in the French guise, with Turkish bows, in hel-
mets of Spanish gold, on good steeds bred in Cas-
tile. Amphiorax is a bishop; Ismene attends
Atys' funeral vested as a nun. Carthage has don-
jon, ditch, and barbican; Troy and Thebes are

mediæval towns. Anachronism is blithely accepted, and elevated to a virtue. Chaucer's plea of extenuation when he arms his Grecian knights with Prussian shields — "there's no new fashion that it was n't old" ("ther nis no newe gyse, that it nas old") — that plea would never have been entered by the French romancers. The obsolete has been calmly jettisoned; the translation into the contemporary is complete.

But there was another metamorphosis even more startling. The mediæval courtly romances of the period were crowded with the marvellous. And the marvellous had built up its own imposing fabric of conventions. And when Benoit and the unknown writers of the other classical romances came to their Latin material, they found there a no less imposing paraphernalia of conventional machinery — the wrath of Juno, the wiles of Venus, the missions of Hermes, the instigations of Pallas Athene. But the gods of Greece and Rome had meantime undergone their *Götterdämmerung*, and the elaborate structure built on their interventions had become to the Middle Ages an empty shell. And so when the epics went over into the romances, for mythology were substituted marvels; in place of the interpositions of gods and goddesses appears the world of magic — magic robes, magic swords, magic tents, enchanted castles and chambers, *fées* and monsters. Above all, the romances revel in a bewildering profusion of *automata* — astounding fabrications of gold and silver and precious stones, in the form of birds, beasts, plants, and men, that behave as if they were alive. In the hall where Æneas and Dido sit down to dine there grows on a trellis of silver a vine of gold, subtly ramified, with grapes of precious stones, and in the vine and on the trellis are ten thousand birds of fine gold, whose least worth is the value of a city. When the wind blows through the branches, the birds all sing, each with its own note, so that from neither harp nor organ issues sweeter sound. Briseida has a robe made through necromancy by an enchanter of India Superior — a robe given by a sage Indian poet to her father Calchas — made partly from skins of sables that dwell in the River of Paradise. But as Benoit himself observes, no one could write on parchment, either in romance or Latin, all its wonders, and I shall waive the enterprise. Those are but two examples out of a hundred. The gods have vanished, and instead the land is "al fulfiled of fayerye."

Nor is it only the gods who have suffered a sea change. The Sphinx, for instance, has been made over in the mediæval image. It was green, states the "Roman de Thèbes" — "green as a leaf of ivy; its head hideous and terrifying, with a nose a cubit long, and great teeth curving to the neck; the teeth that jutted from its mouth curved around till they touched the neck behind. Its eyes were red as a leopard's — no man ever saw so ill-favored a look. . . . But there is still a greater marvel" (so the "Thèbes" goes on); "it covers itself wholly with its ears; its ears are long, and broad, and hairy, and frightful. Its arms are big as a great tent; its mouth black and all its snout; its hands have nails like a lion's. . . . It is clad in a brown mantle, that the *fées* made, fasting." That is the typical ogre of Celtic and French romance, and in the last amazing conception — *fées* weaving, *fasting*, a *brown mantle* for the *Sphinx* — is a compendium of the incredible transmogrification which the mythological conventions underwent.

I shall pass over the displacement of the long-drawn-out epic similes by the pithy and succinct comparisons that our mediæval ancestors, anticipating the modern Imagists, delighted in. For there is a still more significant translation of

conventions in the classical romances that demands attention.

To us moderns perhaps the most extraordinary
phenomenon of the Middle Ages is the mass of
conventions that in literature and life accumu-
lated about *love*. It is not that love itself has
changed its spots. We that are true lovers run
into strange capers still, and certain conspicuous
symptoms of love (the medical term is used advisedly) are as familiar to-day as a thousand
years ago — a lean cheek, a blue eye and sunken,
an unquestionable spirit, a beard neglected, and
everything about one demonstrating a careless
desolation. The difference is this. Through a remarkable series of converging influences — Ovid,
Greek medicine, the exotic oriental doctrines
of the great Arabic physicians — the physical
symptoms of love became in the Middle Ages
established as conventions, pure and simple.
Sleeplessness, loss of appetite, emaciation, pal-
lor, weeping, swooning, restlessness, taciturnity,
aversion to society, were not merely the outward
and visible signs of an inward and spiritual state;
they were, for one in love, good form, to be assumed as such, if one were so unfortunate as not
to be afflicted with them in due course of nature.
They constituted what Chaucer calls the "lov-

eres maladye of Hereos," and Burton elucidates them with a wealth of captivating detail, under the title of "Heroicall Love," in the "Anatomy." That was one set of mediæval love conventions.

There was another, no less conspicuous, but this time social rather than physical in its character. For it involved primarily the attitude of the lover towards his lady. What underlies it holds as good to-day as it did then. But its clothes are different, and in clothes the obsolete is the fantastic. We shall have to touch it very briefly. The most distinctive word in the jargon of the poetry of courtly love is "danger." And danger meant not what it means to-day, but the woman's instinctive difficulty of access, her inexpugnable reluctance to be easily won. And the mediæval lover lived constantly (to use the accepted phrase) in his lady's danger, "held up by the brydel at the [shaftes] ende." Above all, he must *fear* as well as love her. "He who fears not does not love" is an endlessly repeated dictum, and the phrase "love and *dread*" lies thick on the pages of French poetry as autumnal leaves that strow the brooks in Vallombrosa. Moreover, the lover (not the husband; the Middle Ages made sharp distinction there) must *obey* his mistress. She is his "lady sovereyne"; his "earthly god"

("mon Dieu terrien"), to whom he owes unquestioning allegiance. She may send him to the ends
of the earth to win his spurs — "to Walakye, To
Pruyse and in-to Tartarye, To Alisaundre, [and]
in-to Turkye," or even to the mysterious Dry
Sea on the edge of the goblin-haunted sands by
the Jade Gate into Cathay, or farther still, to the
mystic Dry Tree on the "straunge strondes" at
the outposts of the world. I am speaking by the
card; invention were superfluous. "She sent
him," says Chaucer of Arcite's new lady —

> She sent him now to londe, now to shippe;
> *And for she yaf him daunger al his fille*,
> Therfor she had him at hir owne wille.

The principle and its practice are, it happens, not
obsolete to-day. But the bizarre conventional
garb in which this and other tenets of courtly
love array themselves, fill us twentieth-century
moderns, serenely oblivious of our own motley,
with unfeigned wonder and amaze. There, then,
they were, these conventions of love, dominating
and permeating mediæval literature, as they
dominated and permeated mediæval life.

Now love in the classical epics played a minor
part. Wifely love alone marked the "Pharsalia";
the Homeric legends, as they first reached the
Middle Ages, were devoid of love; and it touched

with beauty but a single episode in the "The-
baid." It is only in the great and moving tale of
Dido in the "Æneid" that love assumes a major
rôle. And it was to these epic narratives, for the
most part barren of one of the most powerful
mediæval appeals, that the courtly romancers
came.

What happened? Love was interpolated where
it was not, and translated, where it was, into the
reigning conventions of the day. Dido and Æneas,
in the "Roman d'Eneas," deport themselves in
accordance with the strictest canons of courtly
love. Dido, in Chaucer as in the "Eneas,"
"waketh, walweth, maketh many a brayd, As
doon thise loveres, as I have herd sayd." She
"swowneth . . . dischevele" — as indeed, she
must. I have counted, in a rapid running over
of the "Roman de Troie," thirty swoons of heroes and heroines; in the "Thèbes," twenty-two;
and to swoon four or five times hand running
during a single trying situation is no novelty.
Above all, on the bare hint of the "Æneid," the
innamoramento of Æneas and Lavinia is elab-
orated into one of the most amazing documents
now extant of the very malady of heroic love.
The visit of Julius Cæsar to Egypt in the "Pharsalia" is seized upon by its redactor to introduce,

point-device in its accoutrements, the *liaison* between Cæsar and Cleopatra. But the most remarkable history of all is that of the Trojan story. In the oldest Latin documents there appear, among others, three conventional portraits, of Briseida, Troilus, and Diomede, respectively. They are not brought together, and there is absolutely no story of them in this early work. But, as has been aptly pointed out, given such promising materials as a lady declared to be "affabilis . . . oculis venustis" — "affable, with winning eyes"; one knightly warrior described as "pulcherrimus, pro ætate valens" — "most handsome and valiant for his age"; and a second hero who was, among other things, "cerebro calido, impatiens" — "hot-headed and sudden": granted this starting-point, and the eternal triangle is not far to seek. And so, in the "Roman de Troie," we find the three brought together, and one of the world's supreme love stories launched upon its way — a story into which, before it left the Middle Ages, had been poured the hot blood of Boccaccio's intrigue with Maria d'Aquino, contributions from the exotic romance of "Floris and Blaunchefleur," bits from the affair of Jason with Medea, and finally, Chaucer's matchless insight and humor and felicity of phrase.

In a word, as regards love, no less than mythology and backgrounds, the Middle Ages reclothed the classical epics in the garb of their own day.

But, you say, the garb is ridiculous and has no bearing on the conduct of conventions now. Very well. Let us waive the question of pertinence for a moment and move a little nearer to to-day. The mediæval poetic idiom came after while to seem a jargon — quaint, to be sure, and delectably naïve, but tedious and drolly untrue to life. Dido did n't wallow and swoon, or Æneas wear a helmet equipped with a carbuncle that made the night as bright as day; Troy was n't a second Paris, or Carthage defended by serried rows of magnets that drew steel-armed enemies, and held them, fixed and astonished, to the walls. Let us put away childish things. And so the seventeenth century proceeded to put them away. And in the heroic romances of Gomberville, and Mademoiselle de Scudéry, and La Calprenède, Antony and Cleopatra, Sappho, Cyrus, and Artaxerxes became denizens of the Hôtel de Rambouillet, and later of the salon of the "matchless Orinda" herself. And the quaint eccentricities of courtly love gave place to that sage and serious schematization of passion which found its com-

pendium in the "Carte du Tendre," where the
River of Inclination flowed into the Dangerous
Sea between the Lake of Indifference and the
Sea of Enmity, through rolling country dotted
with the hamlets of Sensibility, and Assiduity,
and Pleasing Verses, and Forgetfulness, and An
Amorous Letter, and Indiscretion. And in such
terms the heroes and heroines of antiquity, no
longer absurdly mediæval but impeccably up-to-
date, discoursed, in one sole novel only, through
six thousand six hundred and seventy-nine deadly
pages. And that was in Molière's century.

But, you still gently insist, it was n't ours.
Well, let us look at ours, and consider the matter
of love alone. What do we do? What, for example, has Stephen Phillips done in "Ulysses" and
in "Herod," and Oscar Wilde in "Salome," and
Hermann Sudermann in "Johannes," and Paul
Heyse in "Mary of Magdala"? There are the
ancient narratives, classical and Biblical, in
which love plays about as slight a part — on the
whole, indeed, a considerably more tenuous one
— than it played in the epics on which the romances were built. And I can repeat, without
change of a word, for the dramas that I have
named, what I said a few minutes ago of the
romances: "Love was interpolated where it was

not, and translated, where it was, into the reigning conventions of the day." The eroticism of
"Salome," of which there is not the slightest
trace in the original, is of a piece with the stuff
of any one of a hundred novels that represent
the vogue; the sexual passion in "Johannes" is
one with the passion in "Das hohe Lied." I am
not passing judgment, either ethical or æsthetic,
on the facts. That is entirely beside the point.
The one thing that concerns us, at the moment, is the fact that we in our way are doing
precisely what the twelfth and the seventeenth
centuries did in theirs — we are reclothing the
same materials in the garb of our own conventions. And I am inclined to think that the
twenty-fifth century (which will have its own
particular modernity to amuse it) will put, for
instance, Oscar Wilde's "Salome" in the same
museum of conventions with the tale of Lavinia
and Dido in the "Eneas," and will catalogue
Aubrey Beardsley's illustrations to the play
with Briseide's mantle and the Sphinx. And when
it comes to the audit before high heaven, it may
well be that the Prioress's smiling that was simple and coy will hold its own with the little
crooked smile of the modern heroine. Let us not
forget our *vade mecum:* "as we are now, so once

were they." Nor is the accompanying *memento mori* in this case without its pertinence: "as they are now, so we shall be!"

Convention, then, is ineluctable. It can say with Brahma:

> They reckon ill who leave me out;
> *When me they fly, I am the wings.*

We escape the conventions behind us only to find ourselves implicated in a new set of our own creating — a consideration which should induce in us large charity towards those limed souls of earlier days who, similarly struggling to be free, were like us more engaged. And that leads directly to a somewhat practical remark. It is this.

The relation in which the *reader* of poetry stands to poetic conventions is radically different from that in which the *poet* stands to them, as he writes. For the poet, the zest of the game lies in his adventures among conventions. Shall he clothe himself in them as with a garment? Shall he impose his will upon them, until form and content coalesce, and instead of an enveloping integument the conventions become bone of his bone and flesh of his flesh? Or shall he grasp their sorry scheme of things entire, shatter it to bits, and then remould it nearer to the heart's desire?

The poet, as he writes, must reckon with conventions as the tools of his craft, the medium of his expression, the impediments that thwart his utterance. His relation to them is immediate, and exigent, and practical. But the reader of poetry is in no such predicament. And in these days when the makers of poetry keep in their *communiqués* the warfare with convention incessantly before us, it is well that the distinction be made sharp and clear. For we who read poetry are ridden and haunted by no such insistent problem, nor are we concerned alone with the coin just issuing from the mint. To us, the old conventions are what the new will one day be — the mould which gives to the very age and body of their time its form and pressure. They represent to us the ways along which beauty has in the past been sought and found, and the very fact that the paths are now deserted and beauty sought no longer where they lead, may lend them a peculiar permanence. An Attic drachma minted in the days of Pericles is no less beautiful because it no longer passes current. Yet, on the other hand, the coin that does pass current must bear the image and superscription of its day. There, in a word, is the distinction which there is some danger that we may obliterate. Those who make

poetry are intent, and rightly, on moulding
it in living forms. But so in their day were all
the poets who have ever lived, from puny whip-
sters to supreme creators. And whatever one
may think about the writing of poetry, its
enjoyment demands a sympathetic understanding
of conventions, whether alive, or dead in the
death that is sometimes the only enduring life.
Sympathetic understanding means, to be sure,
imaginative effort — your true reader of poetry
is always a bit of a poet himself — but the game
is worth the candle. From which brief excursion
into homiletics, let us now return to our sheep.

I have said that from the reader's point of
view imaginative sympathy coupled with knowledge will reinvest old conventions with something of their one-time contemporaneousness.
Here, very briefly, is a case in point. We've been
considering love. Let us turn, for a moment, to
the poem from which we culled the rose-scented
daisy — Chaucer's "Legend of Good Women."
Did you ever stop really to consider who these
"*good*" women were? Or has the spell of the illusion carried unquestioning acceptance with it?
They are, to name the most conspicuous, Medea,
Dido, and Cleopatra, and they are (to quote
no hypothetical objector, but an actual modern

critic who professes English) "they are, as we should say to-day, 'women with a past.'" And that is perfectly true. Cleopatra scarcely lived or died in the odor of sanctity; Medea was the murderess of her children, and of her successful rival; Cleopatra (to round out the tale), of her younger brother, Ptolemy. And Dido was guilty of a flagrant lapse of conventional morality. Why call them "good," and more than that, why actually canonize them, by endowing them with legends, the peculiar prerogative of *saints*? It is a pretty problem in the behavior of conventions. And the reason is as simple as in the case of the daisy, which assumed in verse a fragrance that nature had denied it in reality. Chaucer's century (and by no means that century alone) had a trick of conventionalizing a single person into the representative, the *exemplum*, of a particular attribute or quality. Absalom was the stock embodiment of beauty, Solomon of wisdom, Crœsus of wealth, Hector of prowess, Hercules of strength, Esther of meekness, Penelope of wifely devotion — and so on, *ad libitum*. They were other things, to be sure, as George Washington is something more than the frigid stateliness, and Lincoln than the homespun sagacity, for which they stand to most of us. But the Middle

Ages, with uncompromising thoroughness, sacrificed ruthlessly subsidiary qualities to throw into sharp relief the salient trait, till Griselda, for example, carried patience beyond the utmost bound of human thought.

Now loyalty was in love (as it still remains) the supreme and crowning virtue. And so Chaucer makes

> ... a glorious Legende
> Of Gode Wommen, maidenes and wyves,
> *That weren trewe in lovinge al hir lyves.*

It was as exemplars of *fidelity in love,* in the same category exactly as Penelope and Lucretia and Alcestis, that not only Chaucer, but Boccaccio, and Deschamps, and Christine de Pisan, and the mediævals all and some, thought of Cleopatra and Dido and Medea. Overlooking their weakness, their evil behavior, the poet saw their loyalty alone. The convention lies in the isolation of a single quality from the mass. And on the side of their conventional *form* the "good" women are of a piece with a hundred creations since. They are close kin to the figures of the Jonsonian Comedy of Humors, in whom "some one peculiar quality Doth so possess a man, that it doth draw All his affects, his spirits, and his powers, In their confluctions, all to run one way." They are first cousins to the Micawbers and Barkises and all their breed of Dickens's Human Comedy, who "roll all [their] strength and all [Their] sweetness up into one ball," and live perpetually in singleness of heart, as "willing" or "waiting for something to turn up," or whatever the insulating phrase may be. And last but not least, their congeners by the dozen lie sleeping on the hill in the Spoon River churchyard. The convention is strange and bizarre only when looked at from outside. Once inside it, we're at home; and Medea, despite her failings, is as "good" (to tilt the convention at another angle) as Anna Karenina or Hester Prynne.

But conventions do die. They have, it is true, a disconcerting way at times, like old Roger under the apple tree in the folk-game, of rising abruptly from their graves, and it is never wholly safe to carve their epitaphs. But enough of them are surely dead to warrant a summary statement of how conventions cease to live.

For one thing, conventions die through a process of sloughing off, as new and more vigorous life develops within them. We see it happening in the Moralities, to take one instance only. Here are the conventional virtues — Mercy, Contemplation, Perseverance, Pity, Sapience, Discretion,

Devotion — there are "forty feeding as one," all impeccably correct, "lading out Latin with scoops," in the pithy phrase of an unreconstructed Vice. And among them come leaping the Vices — New Guise, and Nowadays, and Folly, and Mischief, and Free Will, and Ignorance — with their vivid, even lurid Saxon, and their pungent tang of forbidden fruit. What, may I ask, was going to happen when things like the following came into immediate juxtaposition? In "Mankynd" Mercy lucubrates (his spelling stripped of its eccentricities) as follows:

> O sovereigns, I beseech you your conditions to
>   rectify,
> And with humility and reverence to have a remotion
>   To this blessed Prince that our nature doth glorify,
> That ye may be participable of his retribution . . .
>   Mercy is my name, and my denomination;
> I conceive that ye have but a little force in my
>   communication.

"Ay, ay," retorts New Gyse, "your body is full of English Latin"! And here is the way in which he and his confrères in sin discourse:

> Whoop! whoo! lend us a foot-ball.

> Peace, fair babes! Ye shall have an apple to-morrow!

> Beware! quoth the good-wife, when she smote off
>   her husband's head, beware!

Crabbed youth and age can live as well together as those two lingoes. And the staid conventions of the Virtues slip into innocuous desuetude (they would have rolled the phrase as a sweet morsel under their tongues), while the racy license of the Vices heads straight towards Falstaff.

But in the main, conventions die of being used to death. Poets of low vitality ensconce themselves like hermit-crabs, generation after generation, in the cast-off shells of their predecessors. The French poetry of Chaucer's day (to come no nearer home) is possessed of a jargon beside whose deadly yet fascinating monotony the poetic diction of the eighteenth century is kaleidoscopic in its variety. Nor is it the diction only which has hardened into *rigor mortis*. The setting of the vision, the remorseless bead-roll of the catalogues, the stock descriptions whose end is inevitably foreseen from the initial phrase — one feels that the poets relaxed into them and were at rest, as the Bishop at St. Praxed's lay luxuriating in the blessed mutter of the mass, and in the good, thick, stupefying incense smoke. For there is, indeed, something almost narcotic in much mediæval poetry; one is lulled into a pleasing stupor such as one feels in crossing our great central plains, watching from the car window a landscape which always moves yet rarely changes, set for the ear to the steady, monotonous beat of the pulsing wheels. Fitzgerald wrote that Professor Cowell "constantly reads Miss Austen at night after his Sanskrit Philology is done: it composes him, like Gruel." I apologize for even repeating that slander on Jane Austen. But if Professor Cowell had known fourteenth-century French courtly poetry, Jane Austen's occupation had been gone. I confess that I snatch a fearful joy myself in the settled assurance of the sort of thing predestined to confront one when the next page is turned. It comes as near certainty as one attains in this our life. But that shuddering relish for the horrors of conventions at their worst I grant to be a purely human frailty, like a fondness for detective stories. Artistically, the thing is reprehensible, and the feet of it go down to death.

One gets the same thing, too, in the astounding vogues of certain poetic forms — astounding, however, only when one forgets the sonnet cycles, and the heroic couplet, and the short story, and the O. Henry or Rudyard Kipling opening, and *vers libre*. There were the allegories in general and the vision poems in particular; there were journeys through heaven and hell and the underworld (the sentimental and zigzag journeys being yet in the seeds of time); there were temples of this, and mirrors of that. And there was the *débat;* the sort of thing which a little later one finds in the elder Heywood's "Play of Love," that delectable old Interlude in which appeared four characters, of whom one was loving but not loved, another loved but not loving, a third both loving and loved, and a fourth neither loved nor loving. And the amicable debate jogged comfortably on as to which was the more miserable, the "loving not loved," or the "loved not loving"; and which was the happier, on the whole, "both loved and loving," or "neither loving nor loved." There was also beginning what Mr. Lucas recently called "the first effusion of the deplorable cataract of *balades* and *rondeaux*" that swept over Europe. Machaut, Froissart, Oton de Granson, Christine de Pisan wrote them by the score. Of the indefatigable Deschamps I speak with something verging on emotion, for I have twice felt bound to go over the whole four thousand eight hundred eight-line stanzas of the one thousand two hundred *balades* which he alone has left behind — not to speak of the one hundred and seventy-one *rondeaux*, the eighteen *virilais* and the fifteen *lais.* If one wrote at all, one *had* to write *balades*, *rondeaux*, and *virilais*. There were regular rules of the game. Deschamps himself laid them down in all their bewildering complexity, in what Chaucer would have called a "litel thing in prose." It was a test of virtuosity to comply with them. It mattered little what was said; to be formally and conventionally correct was the thing that counted, and that was easiest of attainment, naturally, by slipping as usual into the well-worn verbal commonplaces of the eternal theme of courtly love. Conventions were tyrants as well as servants, then as now.

I have been scrupulously keeping to the Middle Ages. But almost everything that I have said has had its *de te fabula* for to-day. For conventions are shifting, and undergoing metamorphosis, and case-hardening into forms that cabin and confine, now as they were then. But it is hard to estimate justly the significance of their contemporary behavior, because we are caught in the vortex. Critical detachment demands perspective, and we ourselves are in the picture. Yet something approaching perspective may be gained through the recognition of the present in the past. And I have had the present steadily before my eyes in all that has just been said.

There are, then, three determining attitudes toward conventions: we may accept them and passively conform; or we may keep and mould them; or we may gloriously smash them, and go on. Those who passively accept are negligible — *senza infamia e senza lodo*. Neither infamy nor praise is theirs; they are the neutrals in the clash of forces that press outward the frontiers of art. It is the other two that will concern us here: those who accept, but in accepting transmute and re-create; those who reject, and in rejecting strike out for unpath'd waters, undream'd shores. And to the first we may now come.

III

I AM free as the air to-day to coin a vocabulary of
my very own, and speak to you in its fresh-
minted words. I should be thereby, I take it,
"original" in the sense in which many of us
seem to understand the term. Only one thing
stands in my way: I most potently and powerfully desire to be understood by you. You exercise no compulsion whatsoever. If you don't understand, you simply cease to listen. And I, who
am here to communicate, conform. Obviously,
then, the individual is not the only factor to be
reckoned with in what we call originality, so far
as expression is concerned. We express in order
to communicate; to communicate, we must be
understood; in order to be understood, we must
employ the language of those to whom we speak.
That is a fact so obvious that we sometimes
forego the desideratum of putting it on its
inferences.

As a matter of fact, we are all of us original
in our expression until our wings are clipped. I

know a three-year-old boy who calls an automobile a "cadeúga." It is, both to him and in point of fact, an excellently descriptive term, based, like many a word in the pristine days of speech, on the sound the thing makes. But you can't go to the telephone and ask for a "cadeúga" with any valid hope of seeing it appear. And since the world with which the young adventurer must communicate prefers to call the affair a motor, or a car, or a machine (incomparably less exact and fitting terms), he will infallibly drop his own fresh and vivid coinage, and conform. The tangential energy of the individual beats its wings in vain against the centripetal force of the community, and every infant anarchist in speech yields at last to the usage of that world by which, if he is to live, he must be understood.

All this, of course, has larger implications. Expression in art can no more escape the demands of *intelligibility*, than expression in every-day speech. The poet writes in order to communicate, and to communicate he, too, must be understood. And the language of poetry in the broader sense, poetic forms and conventions of whatever sort, is established by long usage, like speech itself. It may, from the point of view of either rhyme or reason, be irrational, even absurd. So are words. But there it is. And though the poet is free as air to create a new poetic language, he takes, if he does, the chances of the youthful coiner of "cadeúga." His own immediate poetic family may understand and marvel, but the world goes on unmoved. What he *can* do is to use the common language with a new distinction, a fresh vividness, a more compelling power. And that offers to originality its richest field.

There are two deep-rooted idiosyncrasies of human nature that bear on our acceptance or rejection of what is offered us. We have, in the first place, an innate bias for the familiar. Whatever we're thoroughly unfamiliar with is apt to seem to us odd, or queer, or curious, or bizarre. For it is no mere trick of speech, but one of those appallingly veracious records of human nature and experience in which the history of words abounds, through which "outlandish" and "uncouth" attained their present meaning. For "outlandish" meant in the beginning only what does n't belong to our own land, and "uncouth" was simply "unknown." The change in meaning registers a universal trait. Whatever is alien to our own ways — the costume, manners, modes of speech of another race or of other times — is strange;

and "strange" itself, which started out by meaning merely "foreign," is only another record of the same idiosyncrasy. That is one thing.

But there is still another trait that is no less broadly human. Whatever is too familiar wearies us. Incessant recurrence without variety breeds tedium; the overiterated becomes the monotonous, and the monotonous irks and bores. And there we are. Neither that which we do not know at all, nor that which we know too well, is to our taste. We're averse to shocks, and we go to sleep under narcotics.

Now both the shock and the narcotic have, I grant, at times their fascination. But they are apt to be forward, not permanent, sweet, not lasting. The source of more or less abiding satisfaction for most normal human beings lies in a happy merging of the two — in the twofold delight in an old friend recognized as new, or a new friend recognized as old. The experience and the pleasure are universal. All the lovers who have ever lived have made experiment of it; a face that you've passed a hundred times, nor cared to see, remains the face you've always known, but becomes all at once the most beautiful and thrilling object in the world; the person you've never known before, you find all at once you've known

from all eternity. Now art, like love, sends its
roots deep into what we are. And our most permanent æsthetic satisfaction arises as a rule from
things familiar enough to give the pleasure of
recognition, yet not so trite as to rob us of the
other pleasure of surprise. We are keen for the
new, but we insist that it establish some connection with what is friendly and our own; we want
the old, but we want it to seem somehow new.
Things may recur as often as they please, so long
as they surprise us — like the Ghost in "Hamlet" — each time they appear.

Let me illustrate what I mean from a single
device of poetry. What is it that charms us in
these stanzas from a fifteenth-century carol?

> He came al so still.
>   There his mother was,
> As dew in April
>   That falleth on the grass.
>
> He came al so still
>   To his mother's bour,
> As dew in April
>   That falleth on the flour.
>
> He came al so still
>   There his mother lay,
> As dew in April
>   That falleth on the spray.

The balance between recurrence and variation is so delicately kept that monotony itself becomes the signal for a fresh surprise. And Poe's consummate and deliberate technique, no less than the limpid simplicity of the carol, secures its almost magical effects by the same means:

> The skies they were ashen and sober;
>> The leaves they were crispèd and sere,
>> The leaves they were withering and sere;
> It was night in the lonesome October,
>> Of my most immemorial year;
> It was hard by the dim lake of Auber,
>> In the misty mid region of Weir:
> It was down by the dank tarn of Auber,
>> In the ghoul-haunted woodland of Weir.

That is but one way out of a thousand in which the familiar merges with the strange. And when a poet, through whatever secret of his art, gives to the expected the thrill of a discovery, he need have no fears for his originality.

What we call originality, then, does not so much consist in the creation of something wholly new, as in this *repristination* (to use Browning's word) of something old. That is not, of course, quite the whole story. But the other side may securely wait.

Let us begin with one or two conventions. And though we start out with the elder poets, we

shall arrive, in the end, at the year of our Lord
that we date by. We have glanced at the dreary
and wire-drawn inventories of feminine charms
in the poetry of courtly love. We should have to
search far to find anything more nearly in the
article of death, and it is worth a moment to see
what could be done towards vivifying it. Here is
a part of Chaucer's description of Alisoun, the
racy young person who lends dubious zest to the
"Miller's Tale." All the familiar paraphernalia
of the stock catalogue are there intact. You begin
with resignation (unless you happen to remember that it's Chaucer you are reading), prepared
for the inevitable — whiteness of *fleur de lis*, red-
ness of roses, smoothness of ivory, clearness of
crystal, grayness of glass; and you find — the
slimness of the weasel, the softness of the wool
of a wether, the shrilling of the swallow's song,
the blackness of the sloe, the fragrance of apples,
the fairness of the pear tree in the spring. The
correct and courtly formulas have gone playing
truant in the fields!

> Fair was this yonge wyf, and ther-with-al
> As any wesele hir body gent and smal. . . .
> Ful smale y-pulled were hir browes two,
> And tho were bent, and blake as any sloo.
> She was ful more blisful on to see
> Than is the newe pere-jonette tree;

> And softer than the wolle is of a wether. . . .
> But of hir song, it was as loude and yerne
> As any swalwe sittinge on a berne.
> Ther-to she coude skippe and make game,
> As any kide or calf folwinge his dame.
> Hir mouth was swete as bragot or the meeth,
> Or hord of apples leyd in hey or heeth.
> Winsinge she was, as is a joly colt,
> Long as a mast, and upright as a bolt.

The hackneyed convention has become vivid as a branch of hawthorn leaves, and racy of good English soil. Let us see what happened to another.

One of the most notorious instances of the mediæval trick of listing things is the so-called *Ubi sunt* formula. It is a comprehensive and detailed interrogation, on the order of "Where, oh, where are the Hebrew children?" as to the whereabouts of all the ancient worthies:

> Dic, ubi Salomon, olim tam nobilis,
> Vel ubi Samson est, dux invincibilis—

and so on through an interminable list. That happens to be from a mediæval hymn, but the thing is everywhere. I shall give at once the most terrible example that I know. Where, asks Deschamps in one of his twelve hundred *balades* — where are David and Solomon, Methuselah, Joshua, Maccabæus, Holofernes, Alexander and

Samson, Julius Cæsar and Hector and Pompey;
Crœsus, King Arthur, Godfrey, Charlemagne,
Darius the Great, Hercules, Ptolemy; where is
Denis the felon king, Job the courteous, Tobias,
Aristotle, Hippocrates and Plato, Judas, Hester,
the good Penelope, Queen Dido, Pallas, Juno,
Guinevere, Iseult, and Helen, fairest of all; where
is Jason, Romulus, Saladin; where he who conquered Aragon, or he who built Avignon, Paris,
Rheims, and Rouen? That is a list from a single
balade only; I spare you two others in a similar
strain. The old convention came to life again only
the other day, in Illinois:

> Where are Elmer, Herman, Bert, Tom, and
>   Charley . . .
> Where are Ella, Kate, Mag, Lizzie, and Edith,
> The tender heart, the simple soul, the loud,
>   the proud, the happy one? —
> All, all, are sleeping on the hill. . . .
>
> Where are Uncle Isaac and Aunt Emily,
> And old Towny Kincaid and Sevigne Houghton,
> And Major Walker who had talked
> With venerable men of the revolution? —
> All, all, are sleeping on the hill.

Herman and Holofernes, Elmer and Aristotle,
Methuselah and Major Walker, Aunt Emily and
Dido — whether it hails from Beauté-sur-Marne
or from Spoon River, the *Ubi sunt* is catholic,

and holds all, quietly inurned. But modern instances aside, the thing with its appalling fecundity dogs one down the Middle Ages in unrelieved monotony. All at once, in France, a supremely gifted poet took it up. He took it up and kept it; but he added one thing — the penetrating beauty of a refrain which fused the dead list into one of the most haunting symbols of human transitoriness:

> Tell me now in what hidden way is
> Lady Flora the lovely Roman?
> Where's Hipparchia, and where is Thaïs,
> Neither of them the fairer woman?
> Where is Echo, beheld of no man,
> Only heard on river and mere, —
> She whose beauty was more than human? . . .
> *But where are the snows of yester-year?*

Sainte-Beuve long ago pointed out that Villon's poignant refrain — his "Mais où sont les neiges d'antan!" — transformed by the alchemy of genius the hackneyed formula. It did. The one compelling phrase became a solvent, through which the hoary banalities of the convention were merged in the fleeting evanescence of all things that are.

Moreover, what Villon did with the *balade* in general is a no less illuminating case in point. He found it more dead than any modern poet has ever thought he found the chrysalids from which the spirits of Tennyson and Arnold and Swinburne have flown. It was a garment walking about with nobody in it. Deschamps in particular had used it as a catch-all for the multifarious sheddings of his mind. His military campaigns, his maledictions on the toothache, his *Weltanschauung* in general, his dislike of tripe, his resentment against England, his observations on different ways of eating, his counsels of perfection addressed to kings and princes, his profound distaste for truffles, his lament for the misfortunes of the church, his views on the seven liberal arts, his lucubrations on the Seven Deadly Sins — all, all, are poured indiscriminately into the *balade* receptacle. It was trite, hackneyed, shop-worn, traditional, bookish, second-hand, ready-made, stereotyped, artificial, rigid — a list of epithets which I have culled from a recent pronouncement of the newer poetry upon the only less new, which has already stiffened, it would seem, in death. The *balade* could cry *peccavi* to these stern indictments all and some. And so Villon found it. The thing he should have done, of course, was to discard it utterly, as fit only for the scrap-heap. He did n't, by the grace of Heaven, and everybody knows what happened. The dead awoke, and not only the "Balade des dames du temps jadis," but "La belle Heaulmière," and a dozen others stand, with vivid and imperishable freshness, among the supreme achievements of poetry.

We might dwell with no less profit upon the progressive desiccation, a little later, of the sonnet. Nobody ever put the reason for what happened better than Sidney himself, who, showing the steep and thorny way to Heaven, on occasion recked not his own rede.

> You that do search for every purling spring
> Which from the ribs of old Parnassus flows,
> And every flower, not sweet perhaps, which grows
> Near thereabouts, into your poesie wring;
> Ye that do dictionary's method bring
> Into your rimes, running in rattling rows;
> You that poor Petrarch's long-deceased woes
> With new-born sighs and denizen'd wit do sing;
> You take wrong ways; these far-fet helps be such
> As do bewray a want of inward touch.

And through these far-fetched helps the sonnet became, in the hands of innumerable practitioners, a thing of frigid conceits worn bare by iteration; of servile borrowings; of artificial sentiment, flat as the lees and dregs of wine. One has only to read *seriatim* the Elizabethan sonnet cycles (with their glorious islets rising here and

there out of the general haze) to find every ear-
mark of the incorrigibly case-hardened convention. Well, Shakespeare responded to the vogue,
and made of the sonnet, with lapses here and
there, the vehicle of the very quintessence of
poetry. "And, when a damp Fell round the path
of Milton, in his hand The Thing became a
trumpet."

But, we are told — and not by recent protestants alone — the sonnet's day is at last done.
Keats wrote that he was "endeavoring to dis-
cover a better sonnet stanza than we have"
— but it is worth observing that he left as his
legacy the realms of gold in the lines: "On First
Looking into Chapman's Homer." "I will never
write another;" Byron declared; "they are the
most puling, petrifying, stupidly platonic compositions." Fitzgerald thought sonnets were fit
only to "serve as little shapes in which a man
may mould very mechanically any single thought
which comes into his head, which thought is not
lyrical enough in itself to exhale in a more lyrical
measure," and that its metre was "a good excuse
for the dull didactic thoughts which naturally
incline towards it." And he also expresses the
pious wish "to tie old Wordsworth's volume
about his neck and pitch him into one of the

deepest holes of his dear Duddon." But through it all the sonnet holds its way. And Rupert Brooke, like Villon, comes along and writes this—of the dead, too, but not "du temps jadis":

> These hearts were woven of human joys and cares,
>   Washed marvellously with sorrow, swift to mirth.
> The years had given them kindness. Dawn was
>   theirs,
>   And sunset, and the colours of the earth.
> These had seen movement, and heard music; known
>   Slumber and waking; loved; gone proudly
>   friended;
> Felt the quick stir of wonder; sat alone;
>   Touched flowers and furs and cheeks. All this is
>   ended.
>
> There are waters blown by changing winds to
>   laughter
>   And lit by the rich skies, all day. And after,
> Frost, with a gesture, stays the waves that dance
>   And wandering loveliness. He leaves a white
> Unbroken glory, a gathered radiance,
>   A width, a shining peace, under the night.

The new comes and takes its place beside the old, and we welcome it. But it is not wise to give up too soon the old for dead. The ways of genius with supposedly cast-off and lifeless forms have to be reckoned with. For the touch of genius is like the miracle of Spring.

Let us return, for a moment, to our thesis. Neither familiar things grown trite, nor things so new as still to be remote and alien, ever grip us as do those things which are at the same time old enough to touch the chords of memory, and yet fresh (if I may use a poet's phrase) with some unspent beauty of surprise. And the supreme test of originality is its power to give us the sense of a footing on trodden and familiar ground, which all at once is recognized as unexplored. That is what Chaucer does times without number. That is what Villon does in the *balade*. For originality, rightly understood, seldom concerns itself with minting a new and particular medium of its own. And genius of the highest order is far more apt to disclose the unexpected resources of whatever vehicle of expression it falls heir to, than to spend itself upon the fabrication of a new.

I know that this is not the doctrine of the hour. And I know, too, that the hour, within due limits, is not without a valid case. "I holde," says that peerless natural philosopher, the Wife of Bath, "I holde a mouses herte nat worth a leek, That hath but oon hole for to sterte to." And originality undoubtedly fulfils itself in many ways. But precisely because the way of creative acceptance is just now more or less anathema, I am doubly anxious, not to defend, but to establish it. The way of constructive rejection shall have full hearing by and by. Meantime, there are certain fundamental and (I believe) still fruitful and operative principles to reckon with.

The current notion that *invention* is a mark of high originality is one of the vulgar errors that die hard. If it were true, "The House of a Thousand Candles" or the "Filigree Ball" would bear away the palm from many a masterpiece. But it is not the case. None of the great poets has ever troubled himself particularly to invent. That is especially true, of course, of narrative and dramatic poetry, and in spite of the fact that both narrative and the drama have now been largely commandeered by prose, the usage of Sophocles, and Dante, and Chaucer, and Shakespeare, and Goethe (although I am far from wishing to conjure with great names) is not without relevance still. They took, then, for the most part, materials that had come down to them — themes that had grown and developed through a selective instinct working, often, through long generations. And instead of inventing, they *discovered*. If that sounds cryptic, let us start with a modern instance that is n't poetry at all.

Dickens, as everybody knows, took over in "Pickwick Papers" a farcical series of sporting sketches, already begun, and intended to centre about a mythical Nimrod Club. In these earlier sketches Mr. Pickwick appeared (*absit omen!*) as a tall, thin man. But before he reached Dickens's hands, by one of those changes on which immortal issues turn, he had become short and fat. And so Dickens found him, and proceeded with his book. And now I quote Mr. Chesterton, lest I be suspected of building up a parallel *ad hoc.* "He made," says Chesterton of Dickens, "in the midst of this book a great discovery. . . . And that discovery constituted . . . the outstanding and arresting original feature in 'The Pickwick Papers.' . . . He had chosen (or somebody else had chosen) that corpulent old simpleton as a person peculiarly fitted to fall down trapdoors, to shoot over butter slides, to struggle with apple-pie beds, to be tipped out of carts and dipped into horse-ponds. But Dickens, and Dickens only, discovered as he went on how fitted the fat old man was to rescue ladies, to defy tyrants, to dance, to leap, to experiment with life, to be a *deus ex machinâ*, and even a knight errant. Dickens made this discovery. Dickens went into the Pickwick Club to scoff, and Dickens remained to pray." So Mr. Chesterton, and in this fashion Samuel Pickwick joined the company of the immortals. And I need not remind you, in passing,

that one Sir John Falstaff, despite his own veracious rehearsal of the circumstances of his birth,
had a not dissimilar pedigree.

Dickens, then, did n't invent Mr. Pickwick; he
discovered him underneath his disguising habili-
ments. And out of his discovery grew a unique
book. There is another unique performance that
grew out of a similar flash of insight. Chaucer
did over into English the story of Troilus and
Cressida as it came to him, particularly through
Boccaccio. He found it an Italianate romantic
epic; he left it the first great English novel.
"Nothing like it," as has been recently said,
"was ever in the world before." How does he
do it?

He starts out in pretty close dependence upon
Boccaccio. And he reaches Cressida herself, and
Pandar. Then all at once something happens,
and you can see it happening before your eyes,
if you read the two narratives together. Some of
you will recall what Stevenson says of "Kid-
napped": "In one of my books, and one only,
the characters took the bit in their teeth; all at
once they became detached from the flat paper;
and they turned their backs on me and walked
off bodily, and from that time my task was steno-
graphic." Well, that is what happened to Chau-

cer. There before him was Boccaccio's Cressida, the conventionally fickle woman. "I came like water, and like wind I go," she might have said, in Omar's words. And the facility with which she went is rivalled only by the fatal ease with which she came. But something else in her seized upon Chaucer, and lifted him, and Cressida with him, bodily out of Boccaccio. And as a result of that flash of vision, a conventional treatment of the hackneyed theme of a woman lightly won and quickly lost, turns into a penetrating and profoundly sympathetic portrayal of the shifting, fluctuating impulses of a woman yielding both against and with her will. And I know no character outside Shakespeare that is at once so human, and so hauntingly elusive in its complexity, or so tragically implicated in the defects of noble qualities, as the Cressida of Chaucer's discovery. What he discovered in Boccaccio's Pandaro, and the matchless figure that he made of it, time fails to tell. But through his fresh conception of what he found in the materials that came to him, he created a new and amazing literary form, and did something that was never done again until Fielding and Thackeray and Meredith appeared.

But Chaucer had the habit of discovering

astounding possibilities in things that appear to
have incurably gone stale. Let us take another
instance. The Middle Ages had a passion for collecting. Jacobus de Voragine, in the "Golden
Legend," collected saints; Boccaccio, in the "De
Casibus," collected tragedies; in the "De Claris
Mulieribus" he collected famous women; the
mediæval preachers were indefatigable collectors
of *exempla*. Story collections, then, were a stock
convention. Chaucer himself had tried his hand
at them more than once. He had done it in the
"Legend of Good Women," and he had done it
in what later came to be the "Monk's Tale."
Indeed, the Monk cheerfully stated, before he
launched into his string of tragedies, that he
had a hundred of them in his cell! Such collections, however, were merely collections — stories
strung together, or confined within some station-
ary framework; tales lifted from their native soil,
and mounted, classified, and pressed in an her-
barium. But stories *grow*. They spring from the
fillip of some suggestion, and one begets another,
and they smack of the qualities of their narra-
tors. A group of men (and I am not forgetting
Chaucer for a moment) are gathered in the
smoking compartment of a Pullman car. The
cigars burn freely, and the bars come down. The

captain of industry lets himself be known by
stories of big business; the soldier has tales of the
trenches; the Californian sings the glories of his
State in dazzling anecdote; the college professor
strives to seem unacademic, but the damned
spot will not out; the commercial traveller tells
the story of his life, and the clergyman discreetly
seeks his berth. Recall, moreover (for you find
Chaucer everywhere), your transatlantic voyages, when such things were. A body of people
whose paths have never crossed before are
thrown together for a week or so without the
possibility of respite or escape. And an act of the
Human Comedy promptly takes the stage. The
boat is scarcely out of sight of land till attractions and repulsions are weaving back and forth.
Like gravitates to like, and propinquity has its
perfect work, to make or mar; total strangers
leave the boat betrothed, and friends of years no
longer speak. Journeys are both fertile soil for
stories, and swift reagents upon human nature.

Now Chaucer knew no Pullman cars nor transatlantic liners, but he did know something that
combined the merits of them both, the pilgrimage. And pilgrims, like their modern counterparts, had their scrips chock-full of news inter-
spersed with lies: "pilgrymes, With scrippes

bret-ful of lesinges, Entremedled with tydinges."
Moreover, pilgrimages threw together, willy-
nilly, every sort of person in the world — "a
companye Of sondry folk, by aventure y-falle In
felaweshipe." And they told their tales each after
his kind, and as they rode they developed antipathies and disclosed affinities. And Chaucer made
the great discovery. *Journeys are where stories
live when they're at home.* Why leave them
stranded in a collection, "lyk a fish that is water-
lees"? And by a stroke of genius he turned a
static into a dynamic thing, and out of a hackneyed literary type the Human Comedy itself
unfolds before our eyes. For if ever the Spirit of
Comedy, with its sage's brows and its slim feast-
ing smile, was luminous and watchful overhead,
it was when the "nyne and twenty in a companye" set out from Southwerk at the Tabard,
on the road to Canterbury. And there, like Cressida, "I take my leve." "Who-so wol here it in a
lenger wyse," says the Monk when he has told
the Tale of Ugolino, "Redeth the grete poete of
Itaille, That highte Dant, for he can al devyse
Fro point to point; nat o word wol he faille."
And what Chaucer says Dante did for Ugolino,
Professor Kittredge has recently done for Chaucer
himself. And the supreme originality of the

"Canterbury Tales" — the matchless give-and-take along the Canterbury road, the self-revelations, the breaking into life of hackneyed narrative forms, when they fall from the racy, or stately, or ribald lips of the pilgrims — all that has been, once for all, devised from point to point, and I shall not retell what has been so luminously told.

I said I should drop the "Canterbury Tales" with that. But I must cast just one more longing, lingering look behind to those warm precincts of the cheerful day. Some of you will remember the incomparable lines in which the Wife of Bath breaks in upon her retrospect:

> But, lord Crist! whan that it remembreth me
> Upon my yowthe, and on my jolitee,
> It tikleth me aboute myn herte rote.
> Unto this day it dooth myn herte bote
> *That I have had my world as in my tyme.*

Well, that is Chaucer's own savoring of life. And that is the secret of his originality. He was original because he could n't be anything else to save his soul. For he was alive to his finger tips, and nothing that he really touched could remain dead. And it is this invincible zest of his, this keen and intimate relish of the Human Comedy — his own rôle with the rest — through which he

vitalizes everything he lays his hands on. He is
everlastingly discovering that dead things are n't
dead at all. He dares to begin the immortal Prologue to the "Canterbury Tales" itself with a
device that had been worn to the bone in the
swarming vision poems of the day. It was always
Spring when the dreamer fell asleep. And the
same conventional birds, trees, and breezes repeat each other, till almost one's spirit dies "for
wo and wery of that companye." How deadly
they were you can only know if, like Chaucer,

> Thou gost hoom to thy hous anoon;
> And, also domb as any stoon,
> Thou sittest at [boke after] boke,
> Till fully daswed is thy loke,
> And livest thus as an hermyte.

But Chaucer as usual saw what others had n't
seen. And he struck through the shell of the trite
springtime convention to the heart of Spring itself. Spring is the time of the irrepressible *Wan-
derlust*, of longings for the open road, over the
hills and far away: "*than* longen folk to goon on
pilgrimages." And so:

> Whan that Aprille with his shoures sote
> The droghte of Marche hath perced to the rote,
> And bathed every veyne in swich licour,
> Of which vertu engendred is the flour;
> Whan Zephirus eek with his swete breeth
> Inspired hath in every holt and heeth

The tendre croppes, and the yonge sonne
Hath in the Ram his halfe cours y-ronne,
And smale fowles maken melodye,
That slepen al the night with open yë,
(So priketh hem nature in hir corages):
Than longen folk to goon on pilgrimages
(And palmers for to seken straunge strondes)
To ferne halwes, couthe in sondry londes;
And specially, from every shires ende
Of Engelond, to Caunterbury they wende,
The holy blisful martir for to seke.

And the pilgrimage is on. And a spirited turn to a jaded commonplace has achieved an opening that is flawlessly organic — and, incidentally, has given to English poetry the lines whose familiarity has kept its April freshness through five hundred years.

Originality, then, is independent of invention. It is rather the gift of seeing and seizing the latent possibilities of familiar things. We accept that formulation without demur when the familiar things are the appearances of earth, and air, and sea, and sky — effects of light and shade, *nuances* of color, aspects of mass and line, sound, fragrance, movement — all the bewildering, iridescent throng of old impressions that all at once flash into new, when the eye is quickened and alert. What we fail, perhaps, to realize is this: that the old and well-worn forms of art, the

familiar treatments of traditional themes, stand
to the poet in precisely the same relation as the
world of eye and ear. And they too may flash into
life under the same compelling vision that at
rare moments pierces the husks of *things*, and
discloses beauty. For art is tradition, and what is
handed down is itself material for the alembic.
It may prove to be utterly intractable, its pristine ductility vanished forever. Well and good;
that is a malady incident to art no less than to
manners and costume and speech. But that is the
other half of the truth — the half that is turned
towards us to-day. What we are concerned with
at the moment is the half that has suffered temporary eclipse: the fact that old forms and old
themes have always remained, and in large
measure still remain, malleable under creative
energy. And what we call originality has always
found rich stuff for its transmutation there.

I shall not summon Shakespeare as a witness.
It is all or nothing with him. One thing only I
shall say. If you wish a complete compendium of
the essentials and the quintessentials of originality, in all their conceivable manifestations, go
on a voyage of discovery of your own, and begin
by reading Lodge's "Rosalynde," and Brooke's
"Romeus and Juliet," and the old "King Leir and

his Three Daughters," and North's noble translation of Plutarch's "Life of Antony," page by page, and sometimes word by word, with the plays that Shakespeare built on them. That is neither a counsel of perfection, nor an injunction to settle Hoti's business; it is a practicable and supremely illuminating enterprise. And forty thousand lectures could not, with all their quantity of lore, make up its sum. For in the firsthand comparison of what Shakespeare found and took with the astounding thing he made of it, lies the touchstone of all originality whatsoever.

There is, however, another question about originality, the answer to which is not without importance. What are the limits of originality, in its sovereign dealing with other men's work?

The problem has been rather hopelessly muddled in our minds through a failure to remember that originality in its narrower sense, as a mere antonym for plagiarism, has always been itself a pure matter of convention. The metes and bounds between "mine" and "thine" in literary property have never remained fixed. They have been, for any given period, determined solely by the current literary usage. And the ethics of the question need concern us only so far as it is a matter of the evolution of conventions. Concern us it must, however, because we persist in judging in accordance with the conventions of to-day older practices, that were subject to a wholly different usage.

The Middle Ages, for example, had practically no sense whatever of literary property, as we conceive it. Rights of possession in other men's work were "free as the road, as large as store." Froissart's words about another matter are applicable here: "there was nothing of which one could say 'It is mine,' for everything was common as the sun and moon." Short of wholesale and servile cribbing, A was as free to incorporate what B had written, as he was to levy on the blessed sun of heaven, for his poetic needs. And it was as little incumbent upon him to state that he had done so, as it is even yet for me to announce that I lifted "the blessed sun of heaven" from Shakespeare. The works of other men, in fact, stood on practically the same footing, to a writer, as the works of God. Chaucer fuses the results of his reading into a new thing, precisely as he fuses his keen and infallible observations of life. And usually he combines the two. The Wife of Bath — who should have lived long enough hereafter to have met in Falstaff her only peer and her only match — the Wife of

Bath herself is simply Chaucer's multifarious
and vivid reading of books, and his alert and
omnivorous reading of life, poured together *con
amore* into the mould of a superbly vital imaginative conception. Now one of the Wife's chief
components happens to be St. Jerome — the most
amazing metamorphosis that ever a saint has
undergone. St. Jerome, however, I suspect would
be the first to waive acknowledgment of such a
borrowing. But the Wife of Bath is no less a debtor
without acknowledgment to one of Chaucer's
contemporaries, Eustache Deschamps. What is
to be said of that? Let Deschamps answer for
himself. Long before the Wife's *apologia pro vita
sua* was written, Deschamps sent across the
Channel to Chaucer, by a common friend, a
remarkable *balade*, the refrain of which is this:
"Grand translateur, noble Geffroy Chaucier"
— Geoffrey Chaucer, *the great translator*. That,
to Deschamps, is Chaucer's distinction; he has,
as it happens, sowed the flowers (it is the *balade*
speaking, and not I) and planted the rosebush of
the "Roman de la Rose" for those who are ignorant of French. But those who are ignorant of
French are also deprived of Deschamps. And so,
in the *envoy*, Deschamps proffers a suggestion.
In Chaucer's garden, he modestly protests, he

would be, to be sure, but a nettle — "En ton jardin ne seroye qu'ortie" — but he makes it unmistakably clear that he was anxious to be transplanted there, if only Chaucer would. And the sequel is this. Chaucer did find in Deschamps, as we now know, stuff for his loom, and wove it into his own tapestry. But it is only within the last dozen years that the discovery was made that he had actually done so. For, in entire accordance with the usage of his day, which Deschamps followed with the rest, Chaucer made no acknowledgment. It would have been a work of pure supererogation if he had. For among that happy breed of men to whom all things were theirs, to take over another's "goodly words" into one's own "douce melodie" was in itself a compliment as acceptable and courtly as any that one could pay. Acknowledgment might or might not be made, precisely as one pleased. And there, indeed, lies the crux of the whole matter. Barring the single point of acknowledgment, originality meant in Chaucer's day substantially what it means now — the transmutation of what is taken over, into something that is essentially one's own. And the difference with reference to acknowledgment grew directly out of the absence of any such active sense as ours of lit-

erary property — an absence which, in turn, was
the result of causes rooted deep in mediæval life.
Our modern sensitiveness to any infringement of
our property rights in the children of our brain
is merely a stage a trifle farther on in the evolution of a convention.

I am not wholly sure, however, that our ethical
gain through the development has not been offset
by an æsthetic loss. At all events, our robust el-
ders in poetry exercised the same imperial rights
of eminent domain over beauty to their liking in
a book, that they exerted over beauty of their
finding in earth, sea, or sky. And the stipulation
of their holding was in either case the same —
they must improve the property. The simile in
Virgil of the souls that fell from the banks of
the Styx like leaves, becomes Dante's property
when he enriches Virgil's lines from his own creative observation; precisely as, no more, no less,
the greenness of new grass becomes inalienably
his when the same penetrating observation con-
fers on it the vividness of fresh emerald the instant it is split. Virgil and the meadow were
alike priceless, and alike legitimate, treasure-
trove. And all this meant, in the end, a splendid
and *cumulative* bodying forth in poetry of the life
of men and things. For poets like Dante, and

Chaucer, and Shakespeare recognized far more clearly and surely than we the perennial vitality latent in *tradition*. And one of their glories is the interpenetration, in their work, of books and life. There they both were; and the creative energy in those more spacious days struck as straight and true for the one as for the other, to find its stuff. And this richness of assimilation of what tradition furnishes gives to the older poetry a body, a fulness of habit, of which we often feel the lack these days, when we all too seldom catch in verse that sense of a rich and varied background flashing into expression in a single poem, or pouring its profusion into the compass of one master work — the sense that sometimes in a single phrase throws windows open upon endless vistas. And qualities like those we can ill afford to miss.

For originality is more than the saying of something never said before about something now for the first time perceived. That has its own high value, we may grant at once; but it has its limitations too. For however exciting it might well be to play a second Adam, and have the Lord God bring to each of us, all new, every beast of the field and fowl of the air to see what we would call them — however thrilling that might be to each happy individual, the universe would not thereby get far. Fresh beginnings are excellent stimulants to a jaded world, but a defective method of progression. The great constructive element in both life and art is the dealings of genius with the continuity of tradition. And poetry becomes original by breaking with tradition at its peril. Cut the connection with the great reservoir of past achievement, and the stream runs shallow, and the substance of poetry becomes tenuous and thin.

This is not an *apologia* for bookishness in poetry. The bookish, the erudite, the academic, are worlds away from what I mean. Cut connection with the other reservoir — "the mighty world of eye and ear" — and the stream again runs shallow, and the substance of poetry becomes this time not merely tenuous and thin, but hard and dead. The vitality of tradition and the quickening impulse of immediate contact with reality — it is the fructifying influence of each of these upon the other that makes for life in poetry. Either without the other means sterility.

Originality, then, is in the main independent of derivation. Its specific quality is the individual stamp: the pervasion of thought and expression, whencesoever derived, by something that

gives distinction, freshness, individuality. Take
a line and a half of Wordsworth's:

> . . . that uncertain heaven received
> Into the bosom of the steady lake.

When Coleridge read that, he sat down and
wrote in a letter: "had I met these lines running
wild in the deserts of Arabia, I should have instantly screamed out 'Wordsworth!'" Of course
he would; they are saturated through and
through with him, — as

> For lo! the New-moon winter bright!
> And overspread with phantom light
> (With swimming phantom light o'erspread
> But rimmed and circled by a silver thread) —

as these lines are permeated with the very quintessence of Coleridge. But,

> An ampler ether, a diviner air,

also bears Wordsworth's unequivocal image and
superscription, though this time the gold is the
gold of Virgil.

For although in life "the rank is but the
guinea stamp, The man's the gowd for a' that,"
in art, where form and content are as indisso-
lubly one as body and spirit, the distinction
fails to hold. It is the cutting of the intaglio that
gives its value to the gem. And "Drink to me

only with thine eyes" is as inalienably Ben Jonson's, by virtue of its chiselled terseness, as if
almost every phrase of it were n't buried in the
letters of a Greek rhetorician; and "Still to be
neat, still to be dressed" is incomparably more
original than a thousand poems that are n't, like
it, the transmutation of the dross of a dozen old
Latin lines into a finished bit of goldsmith's work.
Read some day, when your stomach is strong,
the old song which Burns took over in "John
Anderson my jo, John," and remember, as you
read, that the soaring melody of the rondo in the
Waldstein sonata is Beethoven's similar trans-
figuration of the air of a ribald folk-song about
fleas in straw. For that matter, recall Beethoven's transformations of the conventional minuet
of Haydn and Mozart into that vehicle of rollick-
ing gaiety, and grim mystery, and tragic portent,
the scherzo of the Third, Fifth, Seventh, and
Ninth Symphonies. And in Miss Lowell's "Guns
as Keys: and the Great Gate Swings" — to come
down with a leap to the most modern of the modern — the daring constructive device is no less
original because it gives a brilliant new turn to
what is as old, on the one side, as the "Odyssey"
(in the constant juxtaposition of its great sweep
forward and its waiting goal), and, on another,

of as long date as "Aucassin and Nicolete" (in its alternation of verse and — with apologies! — prose); while from a third angle it's a superb appropriation and translation into words of the methods of the cinematograph. None of these things move us, whether in Wordsworth, or Ben Jonson, or Burns, or Beethoven, or Miss Lowell. They are stuff for the loom, clay for the potter, gold, silver, precious stones, wood, hay, stubble — it matters not what in the slightest degree. We know what they are, but we know not what they may be, when the poet is done with them. For it is n't by the materials you use that your claim to originality will stand justified or condemned; it is solely by the thing you do with them.

There is one other question that will certainly and properly be asked. Where does *inspiration* come in? Is n't it that which, after all, is the true criterion and touchstone of originality? Is it not when, as Goethe puts it, "the good ideas stand suddenly before us like free children of God, and cry out: 'Here we are!'" — is n't it then that we are most authentically original? What, too, of that larger aspect of Goethe's doctrine, which comes so near expressing, once for all, what we each of us would say, if we could, of genius:

Every productivity of the highest type, every significant *aperçu*, every invention, every great idea that bears fruit and achieves results, stands in no man's power, and is exalted above all earthly might. Things that so come we must regard as unlooked-for gifts from above, as veritable children of God, to be received with reverence and with joyful gratitude. They are akin to the dæmonic, which does resistlessly with us as it will, and to which we unwittingly yield ourselves, even while we think we are acting on our own initiative.

Is n't that what we really mean by originality? you will surely ask. Let us see, in the first place, what is not involved.

The ways of genius are as manifold as the mercies of the Lord. Inspiration may spring from what Tennyson calls "unseen germination"; it may come on the spirit, as Keats once wrote, "with a fine suddenness." It may arrive through brooding over an idea and waiting patiently until it shines, as Buffon enjoined. Or it may come in the amazing way in which it came to Mozart: "When I am riding in a carriage, or in a walk after a good meal, or in a sleepless night, then the thoughts come to me in a rush, and best of all. . . . Then [the thing] goes on growing . . . and however long it be, becomes indeed almost finished in my head, so that I afterwards survey it at a glance, like a goodly picture or handsome man; and in my imagination do not

hear it at all in succession . . . but as a simultaneous whole. That is indeed a feast! All the finding
and making goes on in me as in a very vivid
dream." Inspiration may seize on one as "Tam
o'Shanter" seized on Burns, when he walked all
day by the riverside, "crooning to himsel," and
"in such ecstasy that the tears were happing
down his cheeks," as he wrote his verses on the
top of his sod-dyke along the stream. Or it may
weary one, as it wearied Wordsworth: "William
tired himself with seeking an epithet for the
cuckoo . . . William very nervous. After he was
in bed, haunted with altering 'The Rainbow.'
. . . William tired himself with hammering at a
passage." It may come as to Goethe, in his bare
little anchorite's cell of a study, from which (he
says) he scarcely stepped the whole winter
through, except into the still more Spartan bed-
room opening out of it; or it may come as it used
to come to Scott, while he galloped on horseback
over the moors. It may descend as it descended
upon Gautier, working imperturbably in the
midst of the clatter of printing presses; or it may
respond only to cloistral isolation, as with Flaubert: "I'm like a bowl of cream: if the cream is
to form, the bowl must sit immobile." One may
write of pastoral scenery, as Lodge did in "Rosa-

lynde," "in the ocean when every line was wet with a surge"; or one may write of the sea, as Tennyson made "Break, break, break," "in a Lincolnshire lane, at five o'clock in the morning, between blossoming hedges." For inspiration is like the wind, that bloweth when and where and how it listeth. And the modes of its workings are utterly irrelevant to our concern. For Wordsworth tiring himself for an epithet, or Flaubert "afflicting his soul over some dubious word," is as original as Burns gesticulating by the riverside in an ungovernable access of joy, or as Byron dashing off verses after a ball.

But what is it that *sets the winds of inspiration blowing?* That is absolutely the only question that concerns us here. For what we call inspiration, in whatever wondrous ways it may behave once started, always starts. And its starting-point is some concrete suggestion, and that suggestion may be anything. It may be a stubble field under the autumn light, that all at once touches the springs of inspiration; it may be a visit with one's sister to the River Wye, or the bugle music of the boatmen on Lake Killarney, or the nest of a field mouse turned up by a plough. And it may equally well be a line of Virgil, or some phrase of Horace, itself "the birth of some chance morning or evening . . . among the Sabine hills," that in a flash gives wings to the imagination; or a page of "Purchas His Pilgrims," or an old yellow book picked up in a Florentine book stall. The titanic sweep of inspiration through "King Lear," and the thoughts beyond the reaches of our souls in "Hamlet," were stirred to life by two old plays. We are back where we started. What we call inspiration is the dynamic factor in originality — that is all.

Let us end orderly as we began. Poetry may never with safety cut loose from the old, because the old is always new. The tide of generations flows on unceasingly, and for each the old experiences have their pristine freshness. That is why the old themes are perennial. Love is as dazzling a miracle to every lover who loves to-day as if unnumbered millions had n't loved since time began. Death is n't trite to you and me because it 's been the common lot since life first was; nor have the moon and stars grown old because uncounted centuries ago, beside the rivers of Babylon and Egypt, or among the hills and pasture lands of Israel, or in the wide stillness of Arabia, men saw them, and brooded, and wondered, and dreamed. The oldest things in the world are the things that also have been new as many times as human beings have been born. I happened one day this summer to look across at an adjoining cottage. There on the porch was a group of urchins absorbed in constructing a fleet of whittled ships, and on the path below, two little girls, heads close together, each with an arm about the other's waist, oblivious of all but their own secrets. And there, too, was the eternal sea. And each was as old as the other — and as new.

Now that is what the greatest poetry has always built on. Its roots strike deep into the eternally familiar. But the gift of the gods to genius is the power to catch and fix that familiar in the recurrent act of becoming new. That is originality.

IV

THE HARDENING OF CONVENTIONS, AND REVOLT

ART moves from stage to stage, as we have seen, by two opposing paths: the way of constructive acceptance, and the way of revolt. The one is the road of the builders; the other of the adventurers and pioneers. You may prefer one path, and I the other. We shall certainly not all agree on either. But what Chaucer wrote to his little son Lewis is still to the point: "diverse pathes leden diverse folk the righte wey to Rome." And there will always be these two great highways to a common goal, whatever may be your preference or mine. It is because human beings are what they are that the world advances, now by the creative transmutation of the old, now by the discovery and conquest of the new, and now through both together.

For behind our differing attitudes towards conventions stand two fundamental human bents, that between them comprehend the world. There are always souls, the salt of the earth, who say: "So was it when my life began; So is it now I am a man; So be it when

I shall grow old" — who could, and do, wish their days to be bound each to each by natural piety. There are always, on the other hand, restless spirits, who rejoice that man is hurled from change to change unceasingly, his soul's wings never furled. And it is n't to be wondered at that those who live to watch wild ecstasies mature into a sober pleasure, and those who spend their passionate lives in leaps all day to reach the sun, seldom see eye to eye. But the unsolicitous spectator of the game sees both, and sees each as a factor in the paradox of human progress. It would be, I fear, a dull world that developed without break of continuity; it would surely be a mad world that progressed by leaps alone. Neither Wordsworth nor Browning (from whom I strung together my opposing phrases) saw the thing whole. The world and art alike move on through what, in the main, is a continuous evolution, punctuated by the sudden flaming or flowering of a crucial moment now and then. For in poetry, as in the State, it is after all a constitutional régime, tempered by occasional revolution, that remains the least objectionable mode that has been found of muddling through. The amazing scheme of things of which we find ourselves a part demands both conservatives and radicals as indispensable instruments of its unfolding.

We have dealt with the constructive acceptance of the old. And this creative assimilation of what is handed down constitutes the great conservative force in poetry. But the radical attitude towards the old must be reckoned with too. And that attitude is apt to be twofold. It is destructive, because it is tired of the old, and frequently proceeds without compunction to consign it to the scrap-heap. It is also constructive, because it wants the new, and sets forth, not without a cheerful flourish of trumpets now and then, to find it. It is sometimes justified in both procedures; it is usually extreme; and it is always interesting. And without it poetry would indubitably be the poorer.

I propose, then, to consider the radical temper as the complement, no less than the antithesis, of the conservative trend in poetry. But I wish to make my immediate purpose clear. It so happens that we are at the moment in the midst of a period of revolt in poetry. I shall not, however, in this chapter, deal primarily with the idiosyncracies of this particular insurgent movement. Those will be matter for consideration later, for what is going on has quite enough significance to be taken seriously. But it can't be taken seriously, if it is proclaimed as something *sui generis*. It is very far from that. It is an old familiar friend, revisiting, with punctual observance of its period, the glimpses of the moon. And it is this periodic aspect, this background with a long perspective, that is too frequently overlooked. Revolt is perennial, and the best aid to reflection on its meaning now is some acquaintance with its previous behavior. It is with the phenomena of revolt in general, accordingly, that we have immediately to do. The current insurgence will concern us only indirectly.

Let us return for a moment to the type of originality that has already been discussed. It consists, essentially, in a remoulding in fresh forms of old materials. It discovers the new, in other words, as latent in the old, and it finds in existing forms no check upon its own freedom to recreate. Its *cachet* is its power to call breath from the four winds, and breathe upon the valley of dry bones, and make them live. The temper of mind which we have now to analyze finds in the old, on the other hand, a hindrance rather than a help to freedom, and for it the new lies without, not within, the confines of the familiar. Poetry, as the radicals react to it, is shackled by a mass of inherited conventions — dead rhymes, dead metres, dead diction, dead stock ideas. They would play the rôle of Perseus to a new Andromeda, and set the starry prisoner free. Life in poetry, as they conceive it, is a continual sloughing off of chrysalids and trying of new wings. Over against the transmutation of old conventions is sharply set their repudiation in favor of the new. The radical attitude, then, is both negative and positive; not iconoclastic only, but in its way creative too. And it is necessary to regard it from both angles.

We may consider the negative aspect first. The insurgent temper rebels against what it feels to be the dead hand of convention. And it may be granted at once that its revolt is often warranted. We have seen something of the ways of genius in dealing with conventions. But conventions by no means always fall into the hands of genius. More often than not it is poetry's journeymen who ply their trade with them, and then the worst is apt to happen. Let us consider very briefly, then, some of the conditions out of which revolt takes its rise.

The path of least resistance has always shared honors with the primrose way. And the history of conventions offers no exception to the rule.

To touch a trigger and release a formula is easier than to forge and file a thought. If I say "white as" — and stop, nine out of ten of you will instantly complete my phrase by "snow"; a few of you will probably supply "a sheet"; for a smaller, more poetically minded group, the trail leads to "a lily." But beyond "white as snow," "white as a sheet," "white as a lily," few of us will go except by taking thought. If I begin "red as" — most of you have already ended the phrase with "blood," before I pause; a few of you with "fire"; a few with "a rose." "Red as blood," "red as fire," "red as a rose," stand for so many beaten tracks; the cue once given, one goes off at score. And every-day speech and poetry alike are strewn with innumerable phrases which, once started on, conduct us, willy-nilly, along a well-worn channel to an inevitable end. Now most human minds are indolent, and thought is tough. And the temptation to slip at ease along a groove already worn is irresistible. That is why slang is so insidious and so pervasive; it too is a facile surrogate for thought. And the mass of commonplaces and *clichés* that permeate poetry, as they permeate speech, spring in large measure from this inveterate bent of the average mind to follow the line of least resistance. Pope, whose unri-

valled terseness and point have spared countless
thousands the travail of thought on a number of
themes, pays his respects to the "tuneful fools
who haunt Parnassus":

> While they ring round the same unvary'd chimes,
> With sure returns of still expected rhymes;
> Where'er you find "the cooling western *breeze*,"
> In the next line, it "whispers through the *trees*";
> If crystal streams "with pleasing murmurs creep,"
> The reader's threatened (not in vain) with "sleep."

Most excellent fooling! But out of the five occasions on which "breeze" ends a line in Pope's
own verse, in four it punctually rhymes with
"trees." And here are three of them:

> Her fate is whisper'd by the gentle breeze,
> And told in sighs to all the trembling trees.

> In some still ev'ning, when the whisp'ring breeze
> Pants on the leaves, and dies upon the trees.

> The dying gales that pant upon the trees,
> The lakes that quiver to the curling breeze.

With such fatal facility we glide by the canal, or
take the poetic turnpike road! For poetry, after
all, is very much like Harvard Yard. Somebody,
in the good old Colony days, cut across at a new
angle, and another at another, and adventurer
followed in adventurer's wake. And the sequel

to-day of their brave farings-forth is a criss-cross of trim and sacred paths. Which parable he who runs may read — and lo! into the waiting rut I too have comfortably slipped.

There is, moreover, another significant factor in the creation of the conditions out of which revolt is born. It is what we may call the survival of the *un*fittest in conventions. The basic human fact which underlies it meets us everywhere. I recall, for example, one vivid and commanding figure whose tricks of speech and eccentricities of gesture are stamped on scores of men who in the classroom have sat under him, while his vividness and his power remain as inaccessible to their emulation as the moon. Every powerful personality imposes himself inevitably upon a recipient group of followers. But what he cannot give or they receive is the quality that makes him what he is. That is incommunicable. What he can and does transmit is the accidents, the idiosyncrasies, the mannerisms of his genius. And so it comes about that Pope's couplets run wild without Pope's pith and point; that Sterne propagates his inconsequence, while his suavity and ease of style die with him; and that Byron's rhetoric rolls on, bereft of Byron's "daring, dash, and grandiosity." The slopes of Parnassus are crowded with poets clad in the cast-off accidents of genius.

And so, when dead conventions squeak and gibber in the streets, there are just three ways of reckoning with them. Poets may set the conventions going with the detachment of a phonograph, and even absent themselves, to all intents and purposes, entirely. Or they may exercise creative energy, as we have seen, upon dead forms and empty shells, and bring about a metamorphosis. Or, finally, they may rise up in revolt, repudiate the old coinage altogether, and more or less definitely set themselves to minting new. And the last procedure is as common, and as inevitable, as the other two.

For artistic reactions move in cycles. In perpetual alternation the same tendencies emerge, give rise to their opposites, are supplanted by these opposites, and out of that very eclipse emerge again, to undergo like metamorphosis. And there is a certain cosmic humor in the recurrent shift by virtue of which the rebel, in due course, becomes the conservative, the older freedom a new tyranny — when the cycle automatically starts again. The way to perfection, as Pater declares, is through a series of disgusts. And it is an inveterate habit of English poetry, once in so often to be stricken with conviction of sin, and — in the words of the catechism — to turn from it, with full purpose of, and endeavor after, new obedience. For the excesses of verse, no less than those of frail humanity, carry in their wake the inevitable reaction, and the history of English poetry is an illuminating record of periodical farewells to folly. The poetic aberrations of the seventeenth century (broadly speaking) led to a sharp revulsion of feeling and practice in the eighteenth; against the tyranny of the mid-eighteenth-century conventions, the late eighteenth and the nineteenth century rose in revolt; and now the air is vocal with the battle-cries of the young insurgents of the twentieth. The wheel has simply come full circle, and they are here — till the moving wheel turns on again! For any revolt — this, that, or the other — is merely one of the countless waves of action and reaction between which the arts, like life, perpetually swing to and fro, and, through an occasional ground swell, sometimes farther on.

And that brings us to the positive aspect of revolt. With the spirit of the rebel there often goes hand in hand the spirit of the pioneer. For we obviously cannot forever merely transform and retransform the old. If poetry is not to become a stagnant pool, there must also be fresh influx of the new. But in our preoccupation with the trodden paths, most of us remain oblivious to the vast tracts of the unexplored, which lie waiting to be drawn within the circle of the known, and so, and only so, to become the plastic stuff of art. Now poetry, which attains its highest triumphs in the transmutation of the familiar, is also everlastingly reaching out, for new substance for its alchemy, into the regions of the strange. It has always done it, and presumably it always will. It may, and frequently does, make shipwreck in the process. But it also may, and frequently does, bring back from whatever new lands it has spied out at least the promise of enlarged possessions. It takes even chances, when it sets out, of shipwreck or of spoils. But neither the race nor its poets would have got far without a certain ardor in the blood that leaps at chances, and that adventures to the shores washed with the farthest sea.

Nor need we vex our souls particularly over the vagaries of the voyagers. The inevitable extremes are merely insurgency's alms for oblivion. The essential point is that a residuum persists; a new inch of the strange has been made familiar; and the frontiers of art have been so far ad-

vanced. And when the Kandinskys and Stravin-
skys, the Picassos and the Matisses, futurism
and cubism, and all the other isms that make
the recent history of art read like a series of
bulletins from revolutionary Russia — when
these have enjoyed their nine days' wonder, and
been gathered to their fathers, the technique of
art is usually found to have gained a little in
finesse and flexibility, and our recognition of
beauty to have been appreciably widened in its
scope. For after the pioneers there follow others,
when the strange has become no longer strange,
who transmute what the adventurers have
brought within the circle into something that
is enduringly old and new in one. And in the
fact that it makes this ultimate transformation
possible lies one of the outstanding glories of
revolt.

The insurgent temper, accordingly, supple-
ments, even while it apparently contravenes, the
spirit that busies itself creatively with forms and
themes that have been handed down. The irony
of revolt, to be sure, lies in the inability of the
new to remain the new for more than a fleeting
moment. The less commonplace it is, the more
eagerly it is seized upon, and the more swiftly
and surely worn trite. The *cliché* is merely the

sometime novel, that has been loved not wisely but too well. Yet none the less, the highest boon which the new can crave of the gods will always be the chance of becoming old. For the old will perennially become new at the hand of genius. That is the paradox of art, and likewise the reconciliation of conservatism and revolt.

I trust that I have now made clear my conception of the function and the value of revolt. For I am anxious not to be misunderstood as captious or censorious in pointing out certain tendencies inherent in the radical procedure, which constitute not so much a menace to poetry as an efficacious mode of suicide for their practitioners. The devotion of insurgency to the principle of neck or nothing (a devotion which is one of its engaging qualities) carries certain fairly uniform consequences in its wake. And just now an unprejudiced appraisal of the pros and cons together may not be without its value. A discussion of either without the other, whether it be panegyric or tirade, is futile.

In the first place, there is one general principle which it is important to emphasize. Revolt, in the nature of the case, suffers under a specific limitation. Its own character is in large measure determined by that against which it is directed.

The new must not only not be that, but it must be different. And, as a rule, the aim of revolt is to be as different as possible. Action and reaction, in poetry as elsewhere, are apt to be equal in intensity and opposite in direction. The thing against which we protest exercises its compulsion upon us even in our act of protest, and no declaration of independence can ever be itself quite free. Moreover, human nature is so constituted that the mental state accompanying protest intensifies itself by a sort of auto-intoxication, and grows by what it feeds on. "The French," said Goethe, speaking in 1830, "at the beginning of their present literary revolution, were after nothing further than a freer form. They could not stop with that, however, but threw overboard, along with the form, the previous content too." And that verdict is borne out by the history of practically every literary revolt, before or since. The tendency, inherent in human nature in its protesting moods, is (if I may spoil the Egyptians of a proverb) to throw out the baby with the bath. And even when it does not adopt that simple but extreme procedure, revolt is still restricted, now more, now less, by the conditions that gave it birth. It is not a free and independent, but a contingent phenomenon. And that is a fact which we shall need to bear in mind.

It confronts us at once when we approach the revolutionary notion of *originality*. The type of originality which we have already analyzed, and which exerts itself in the creative transformations of old forms and of familiar themes, is anathema to the insurgent bent of mind. The determining factor in the insurgent quest of originality is a fine impatience of the stereotyped and second-hand. The element of recoil becomes at once the dominant influence, and the would-be original veers perilously towards the extravagant and the eccentric.

It does so largely, and it always has, because of a very plausible and quite intelligible frame of mind. The old things have all been said; there is nothing left us but to say new things, or else to give to what has already been said some dazzling or sharply arresting turn. We run across the feeling unmistakably after the great Elizabethans and Jacobeans had left the platter bare. "We acknowledge them our fathers in wit;" writes Dryden, "but they have ruined their estates themselves, before they came to their children's hands. There is scarce an humor, a character, or any kind of plot, which they have not blown upon. All comes sullied or wasted to us. . . . This therefore will be a good argument to us, either not to write at all, or to attempt some other way." And in different words, but to the same effect, the twentieth-century artist heroine of Eden Phillpott's "Banks of Colme" speaks to the question: "Just because [art] can't surpass [the old masters], it wants to find new channels and be different. It wants to say new things in a new language that's never been used by art before. . . . We don't want to say again [what's been supremely well said]. . . . We want to say something new." That is a desire with which even a lecturer can poignantly sympathize, but alas! there are lions in the way. For the world is very, very old, and back in the caves of the Pleistocene, art began saying things, and it's kept at it ever since. And now to say something in a way that shatters the moulds and discloses a marvel is n't, as old Thomas à Kempis says of self-abnegation, "*opus unius diei, nec ludus parvulorum*" — it's neither child's play, nor will the labor of a day suffice to reach it. Now and again some lucky mortal does the trick, and that is a red-letter day for poetry. But since the desire and its expression spring eternal, while the visitings of genius touch endeavor only at rare and fleeting moments, the upshot of the effort, for the most part, is a more or less violent straining after the unusual.

Now this striving after a salient individuality of expression coupled with the spice of novelty, leads poetry, on occasion, to play fantastic tricks before high heaven. We are endeavoring to reach clearness about the quality of revolt in general, rather than to lay stress, at the moment, on the insurgency that holds the stage. Let us go back, accordingly, to some earlier exemplifications of the same tendency.

There is, as it happens, a singular phenomenon which we may designate as spurious originality. It retains the old conventions, but instead of transforming them, it strains them, as Celia would say, out of all hooping. It works by distortion rather than by transmutation, and its practitioners aim at novelty by the happy expedient of each going the other one better. The lady's eyes kindle the flame of love in her adorer's heart. That is an immemorial convention. But it becomes trite and commonplace. One of the Italian fifteenth-century *concettisti*, Tebaldeo, improves upon his predecessor Cariteo, takes the convention, and twists it into a more arresting form. His lady's house one day takes

fire. Her friends rush up with buckets of water —
all in vain! For the fire from the lady's *eyes* compels the would-be rescuers to dash the water, not
against the burning house, but in self-defence on
their own now flaming breasts. Barnabe Barnes,
an Elizabethan sonneteer, achieves another con-
tortion:

> [My passions], when the Taper of mine heart is
>   lighted,
> Like Salamanders, nourish in the flame.

Robert Tofte, Gentleman, tells how

> On quicksedge wrought with lovely eglantine,
> My Laura laid her handkercher to dry;
> Which had before snow-white ywashed been.
> But after, when she called to memory,
> That long 't would be before, and very late,
> Ere sun could do, as would her glistering eyes:
> She cast from them such sparkling glances straight,
> And with such force, in such a strangy guise,
>   As suddenly, and in one selfsame time,
>   She dried her cloth; but burnt this heart of mine.

The Elizabethan sonnet-cycles are a treasure-
trove of conventions, distorted, in a mistaken
endeavor to galvanize them into life, into sheer
grotesquerie. Their last state is worse than the
first, as a *danse macabre* is more fantastic than a
quiet corpse.

The natural recoil from the commonplace, in

other words, is towards the *singular*. Not only must we be spared the obvious at all hazards, but unexpected and remote analogies must startle us incessantly. And there is perhaps no more salient instance in English poetry of this revulsion from the conventional to an unchartered individuality of expression than the case of John Donne. For here was one of the most daring and penetrating imaginations, one of the most subtle and restless intellects that ever, before or since, expressed itself through the medium of verse. Yet for all his magnificent and lavish gifts, Donne is the preëminent example of the inability of genius itself to escape the inevitable, when a dominant individuality refuses to be subdued to what it works in, and rebels against the limitations imposed upon every one who would impart his thoughts. Donne imagines (or recalls) a flea, in which his own and his lady's "two bloods mingled be." "Oh! stay," he cries,

> . . . three lives in one flea spare,
> Where we almost, yea, more than marry'd are.
> This flea is you and I, and this
> Our marriage bed and marriage temple is.
> Though parents grudge, and you, we're met,
> And cloister'd in these living walls of jet.
>> Though use make you apt to kill me,
>> Let not to that self-murder added be,
>> And sacrilege, three sins in killing three.

But ideas that essentially belong asunder cannot, even at the hands of genius, be permanently joined together, and the shock of surprise once over, we wonder at an amazing and perverse ingenuity, and pass on. And in Donne at his worst, the passion for singularity contorts, through its excess, both stuff and form into the fantastic. Yet he has also left, along with profoundly imaginative poems, imperishable lines: "I long to talk with some old lover's ghost Who died before the god of love was born"; the famous characterization of "her pure and eloquent blood"; and that supremely characteristic interpenetration of Love and Death and Beauty in one haunting phrase: "a bracelet of bright hair about the bone." But those lines of his which live, survive by virtue of a transcendent and unique originality of another type, which works through pervasion, not distortion, and which leaves what it touches strangely, it may be even eerily, luminous. The others coruscate like brilliant pyrotechnics — and go out.

But Donne did not and does not stand alone. Richard Crashaw, for example, in "The Weeper," lets himself go in a wild flight after new images to express the Magdalen's weeping eyes, and the result is a *locus classicus* of seven-teenth-century conceits:

> Hail, sister springs!
> Parents of silver-footed rills!
> Ever-bubbling things!
> Thawing crystal! snowy hills!
> Still spending, never spent! I mean
> Thy fair eyes, sweet Magdalene! . . .
>
> Such the maiden gem
> By the purpling vine put on,
> Peeps from her parent stem,
> And blushes at the bridegroom sun.
> This wat'ry blossom of thine eyne,
> Ripe, will make the richer wine.

And so through eighteen incredible stanzas up to this:

> And now where'er He strays,
> Among the Galilean mountains,
> Or more unwelcome ways;
> He's followed by two faithful fountains;
> *Two walking baths, two weeping motions,*
> *Portable, and compendious oceans.*

It's as if a lunatic had propounded a series of conundrums: "Why are the Magdalen's tears like grapes? Why are they like cream? Why like snowy hills? Why like nests of milky doves?" And Crashaw plies his ingenuity to answer them. Yet Crashaw's no less is the sheer magnificence of the closing apostrophe of "The Flaming Heart":

O thou undaunted daughter of desires!
By all thy dower of lights and fires;
By all the eagle in thee, all the dove;
By all thy lives and deaths of love;
By thy large draughts of intellectual day,
And by thy thirsts of love more large than they;
By all thy brim-filled bowls of fierce desire,
By thy last morning's draught of liquid fire;
By the full kingdom of that final kiss
That seized thy parting soul, and seal'd thee
    His —

and so on to the close of the splendid lines. The absurdities of "The Weeper" are merely originality gone astray, seduced and obsessed by the mania for novelty at any cost.

The discovery of the circulation of the blood was, I suppose, a theme worthy of the lyre. Anyway, Cowley thought so. And in his "Ode upon Dr. Harvey" he depicts the discoverer as hot on the scent of nature — "coy nature," who

When Harvey's violent passion she did see,
Began to tremble and to flee . . .
What should she do? through all the moving
    wood
Of lives endow'd with sense she took her flight:
Harvey pursues, and keeps her still in sight.
But as the deer, long-hunted, takes a flood,
She leap'd at last into the winding streams of
    blood;
Of man's meander all the purple reaches made,
  Till at the heart she stay'd.

Once there, she incontinently boasted of her safety:

> She spoke: but ere she was aware,
> Harvey was with her there —

and there I leave them! "Thise cookes," cries the Pardoner in the "Canterbury Tales," "how they stampe, and streyne, and grinde, *And turnen substaunce into accident!*" Than which I know no terser summary of the procedure of what I must once more call originality gone astray.

I have gone back to the seventeenth century, because it is perspective that we are seeking. But the tendency, *mutatis mutandis*, is not confined to any period. And most of the worst of our own so-called "New Poetry," and occasionally some even of the best, is characterized by this same straining of expression, often to the breaking point, in its ardent quest of the striking and the novel as a recoil from the threadbare and the trite. The tendency to rebound from that *bête noire*, the *cliché*, into the far-fetched and the extravagant, is there, and it is unmistakable. And now, as always, its indulgence is an expeditious way, to court mortality. And many of those who follow it deserve a better fate.

"I think," wrote Keats in one of his letters, "I think poetry should surprise by a fine excess, and not by *singularity*." There, infallibly touched, is the distinction which poetry insurgent is apt to overlook. A fine excess is not only not inconsistent with poetic truth; it may even be part and parcel of it. Singularity intrudes *itself*, and shatters the illusion. It does more. And Keats hints at its fatal defect in his next words: "[Poetry] should strike the reader as a wording of his own highest thoughts, and appear almost a remembrance." For poetry may never with safety cut wholly loose from what is common to the poet and the rest of us. Subject to that, it may be as individual as it pleases. But as individuality approaches singularity, it retreats from its lines of communication, and isolates itself. And that way disaster lies.

For there are always, as we have seen, two parties to all communication of whatever sort — the individual who speaks, and the community to whose usage he must conform, if understanding is to follow. It is the hall-mark of the conservative temper that it never loses sight of the community by which it would be understood. At its worst (and its worst is very bad), it conforms with entire and slavish acquiescence; at its best, it enters into an intimate partnership, following, while at the same time it leads. But the tendency of revolt is to let the community go hang, and to be at all costs itself. And precisely to the degree in which the purely individual as such thus isolates itself, it dissolves the partnership out of which permanent and fruitful understanding grows. For the problem of all great expression in art reduces itself to this: to the striking of the supremely difficult and delicate balance between the contribution of the individual and the contribution of the mass, of which he is, whether he will or no, a part. Overbalance the nice adjustment on either side of the scale, and loss is the inevitable result. Throw the weight overwhelmingly on the side of conformity with the usage of the community, and freshness and vitality flee away, and the thing that has been goes on to be, till the end of the chapter. Throw it overwhelmingly on the side of the sharp projection of the individual, and the resulting saliency strains, if it does not break, those lines of junction with the community which are the *sine qua non* of intelligibility and acceptance.

The characteristic of revolt which we have just discussed has to do rather with form than with content. But the insurgent temper rebels against threadbare themes, precisely as it repudiates hackneyed expression. And here as there, it sets out in quest of new. Let us turn, then, to its dealings with the subject-matter of poetry.

We are perhaps in some danger, in our purely academic preoccupations, of forgetting that poetry behaves as it does, because people are what they are. And revolt in poetry is not a wind that blows aloof and fitfully along the upper reaches of the air. It is bound up with the general ebb and flow of attractions and repulsions which go to make up life. And it is never amiss to begin by scrutinizing life, when one is questioning the ways of poetry.

Now life, as we all agree, is a mass of more-than-Chestertonian paradoxes. And none of them is more curious than that twofold attitude of ours towards the familiar and the strange, which we have already had occasion to observe. For stable satisfaction we most of us settle down in the familiar. But we are all, at the same time, creatures of reaction, "with what we most enjoy contented least." Too long a siege of the familiar without mitigation sets us hankering after the strange, as William James, in the midst of the irremediable flatness of Chautauqua, found himself longing for "something primordial and savage, even though it were as bad as an Armenian massacre, to set the balance straight again" —

for that element of precipitousness, as he calls it, which gives its picturesqueness to the wicked outer world. On the other hand, give us a protracted sojourn in the exotic and the alien, and there descends upon us an overwhelming, even passionate homesickness for the familiar. "Da wo du nicht bist, da ist das Glück" — that piquant dictum holds the keys to æsthetic reactions, as well as to the more homely human sort.

For deep in the paradoxical heart of all of us is the perennial longing to be what we are not. Jaded and oversophisticated denizens of towns devote themselves to pastorals; Marie Antoinette and her court play shepherds and shepherdesses at the Trianon; Horace Walpole turns Strawberry Hill into the fearful and wonderful thing that he thought was Gothic; and the watchword of a land of cities is "Back to the farm." And all that, I suppose, is the secret of the lure of the unknown, which has exercised at times a more or less compelling influence on poetry. The unexplored is, for the moment, where we are n't, and therefore where, for the moment, we want to be. Let it once cease to be unknown, and paradox reasserts itself, and the glamour fades. But that comes later. And one of the symptoms of revolt in poetry is the appearance, side by side with its respectable, burgher-like, work-a-day themes, of more or less outlandish strangers. And when the fit is on, the remote in space, the distant in time, and the recondite and occult in human nature alike attract the insurgent temper. Let us glance briefly at but one of the three.

One of the most illuminating chapters in the history of art — and I do not know that any one has fully written it — would be that which dealt with the gradual drawing of the strange in *space* within the purlieus of the familiar. For the remote in space has always had the faculty of stirring that shuddering pleasure which springs from what, in equal parts, we shrink from, and w⁴ want. The lure of the thing is exercising its old potency afresh to-day, in manifold forms. But since restriction is imperative, I shall confine myself to the spell which has always been thrown over poetry by the Orient, especially since that happens to lend itself to a further use. For the influence of the East has gone through stages that are perhaps of some significance.

The most vivid record of that fascination which I know is found in the mediæval *Mappemondes* — those *images du monde* in which Europe, Asia, and Africa lie folded close together, three cells within the circle of the Ocean Stream, like the

embryo of the later world. For there, on the sides
of the North, and especially in the unfathomable
East, were set down all the dreams the Middle
Ages ever dreamed — the shadowy and fabulous
Pentexoire, the land of Prester John, where the
mediæval fancy revelled in the most engaging
set of marvels that even it conceived; the Castle
of Gog and Magog, just across from where Japan
now lies; not far from it, the Land of Femenye;
in easy reach of that, the Earthly Paradise itself
— and so on endlessly. And back along the mysterious trade routes, stretching dimly into Central
Asia, came bits of fact that were speedily meta-
morphosed into new marvels, until the maps with
their legends, and their accurately pictured gob-
lins and demons and monsters, became a veritable repository of the illustrated fiction of their
day. All that in drab reality was not, received a
local habitation and a name to conjure with, just
across the frontiers of the known. And poetry
seized upon its opportunity, and what we have
seen in the classical romances, with their child-
like zest in the marvellous, is one of innumerable
embodiments of the same ineradicable tendency.

Then gradually the unknown East became familiar. And it is possible to watch the glamour
fading on the very maps themselves. John Speed,

at once cartographer and worthy member of the
Merchant Tailors' Company, had on his map of
China, of 1626, beneath the ghoul-haunted Desert of Lop, the cautious legend: "Where men are
thought to be seduced by wonderful illusions and
deuilish spittings." But Speed had moments
when his faith was wholly dry. For on his map of
Tartary, near the head of the River Ob, appears
this quite unpunctuated record of his disillusion-
ment: "Pliny places the perosites here whom hee
saith be so narrow-mouthed that they live only
by the smel of rost meat beleeve it not." And so
John Speed became a convenient index of the
general fading of this special vision into the light
of common day. Even by Marlowe's and Shakespeare's time the Orient, as a *terra incognita*
where the fantastic had free rein, was largely
of the past.

But it had lost its first hold only to catch imagination in a yet stronger toil. The Orient known
became more profoundly unknown than before,
though in a different way. It had ceased to be
the haunt of naïve and fantastic marvels, but it
had come to be, as it still remains to us Occiden-
tals, seductive with all that is cryptic and unfathomable in humanity itself. "The mysterious
East faced me," wrote Conrad in "Youth,"

"perfumed like a flower, silent like death, dark like a grave." And I cannot serve my purpose better than by quoting the unforgettable continuation of the passage, in which the Orient, silent, impassive, and motionless, looks down in the morning at the shipwrecked boats come up from their tussle with the sea: "And then I saw the men of the East — they were looking at me. The whole length of the jetty was full of people. I saw brown, bronze, yellow faces, the black eyes, the glitter, the color of an Eastern crowd. And all these beings stared without a murmur, without a sigh, without a movement. . . . Nothing moved. The fronds of palms stood still against the sky. Not a branch stirred along the shore, and the brown roofs of hidden houses peeped through the green foliage, through the big leaves that hung shining and still like leaves forged of heavy metal. This was the East of the ancient navigators, so old, so mysterious, resplendent and sombre, living and unchanged, full of danger and promise." And that is the East which has exercised its spell upon Occidental poetry for centuries — on Goethe, and Rückert, and Heine; on Flaubert, and Baudelaire, and Gautier; on Marlowe, and Byron, and now, very particularly, on the poets who are writing at this moment. And they are doing both an old thing and a new thing.

On the one hand, what is happening to-day is what has happened again and again through the long and checkered career of poetry. For whenever poetry finds the uses of its special world gone flat and stale, it is very apt indeed, before the reaction runs its course, to turn its eyes to the exhaustless East. And that is what it is doing now. But the interesting thing is that it is doing it in a fashion entirely in keeping with its own peculiar tendency. It is n't the vastness or the mystery of the East that this time exercises its old compulsion. For very modern poetry has set its face like a flint against all vastness and mystery whatsoever. These are among what it would call the "cosmic" qualities, and from the cosmic its very soul revolts. That which does allure it in the East is an amazing tininess and finesse — the delicacy, that is to say, and the deftness, and the crystalline quality of the verse of China and Japan. Bits of *chinoiserie,* and Japanese jewels five-syllables-long are our chief modern treasure-trove. And all that is as inevitable as gravitation. If you happen to be rebelling against what you regard as too much soul in poetry, you can't be expected to set out forthwith in quest of the illimitable. And that is why a new and significant phase of the immemorial Oriental influence is coming into English poetry. And so far that is pure gain. If you or I happen to prefer an East perfumed like a flower, silent like death, dark like a grave, the East of the mystery is still there. For in our rebellion against rebellion we sometimes overlook the fact that poetic revolution, unlike civilized warfare, leaves unmarred the objects even of its deep antipathies. Meanwhile, it is as idle, in the present instance, to quarrel with a predilection for the intense compression of the *hokku*, for example, because its sharp terseness does n't loom vast and vague, as it is to object to a squirrel because it's not a mountain:

> If I cannot carry forests on my back,
> Neither can you crack a nut.

And I strongly suspect that deftness and precision are an asset of high value to poetry just now. At all events, if the technique of Oriental verse enriches European poetry as the technique of the Oriental graphic arts has enriched European painting, this particular excursion beyond the bounds of the familiar will not have been a mere vagary. And in things like Mr. Fletcher's "Blue

Symphony," and the magic casements opening into old Japan in Miss Lowell's "Guns and Keys," one feels that new achievement is not far off.

But to say that is not to say all. I have chosen deliberately the attitude of poetry towards the Orient, because that happens to be conveniently symbolic of changes that have been, unless I am mistaken, coming slowly over the character of revolt itself. For more and more the spirit of revolt, in its successive manifestations, has been undergoing sublimation, if I may put it so. The strange, the remote, in its larger, more broadly human aspects — and by that I mean such universal qualities as in the older influence of the Orient stirred the imagination through the appeal of mystery, or spoke to the spirit of adventure — all this has-been gradually losing its hold upon poetry. Instead, when we fly from the obsession of the familiar, it is growingly apt to be to the more recondite, or precious, or quintessential, or even perverse embodiments of the strange or far — to "the special, exquisite perfume" of Oriental art; to beauty that is "the deposit, little cell by cell, of strange thoughts, and fantastic reveries, and exquisite fancies"; to the exceptional and the esoteric, in a word, rather than to the perennial and universal. That was the trend of the *Symboliste* movement in France; it characterized the "naughty nineties" in England, and *fin de siècle* art in general; and some of the very best of the poetry that is being written now is moving in the same direction. That means gain, I repeat without the slightest hesitation. For the present tendency of poetry to "quintessentialize," as Henley called it, enriches, without cavil, the interpretation of life through art. But to grant that does not release us from the endeavor to attain perspective; and looked at in perspective, one or two salient facts stand out.

There is, for one thing, a striking tendency of latter-day revolt, which is a corollary of the phase that we have been discussing. I have spoken of the individual poet in his relation to the community by which he must be understood. But the very term "community" is now ambiguous. A community is a body of people bound together by common interests and a common medium of communication. And when poetry began, all those to whom it was addressed had, as a matter of fact, all their interests virtually in common. But what we're pleased to call civilization has profoundly modified the old conception. The larger community, which was once the only one, is split up into a complex of intersecting circles that represent the rise of innumerable special interests. There is, of course, an area common to all the circles — an area in which all men still meet on common ground; there are smaller areas common to a number of the circles, but not to all; and there are tracts which fall within the circumference of one circle only. And the growing disposition of revolt is to strike away from the common centre to the special areas that lie out towards the periphery. In other words, the tendency of poetry to quintessentialize, results in a narrowing of its audience from the whole community to the *élite*, and the poetry of revolt is apt to become the poetry of a coterie. That was true of *Symbolisme;* it was true of the activities of the nineties; it is true, with certain large qualifications, of the insurgent movement of to-day.

All this carries with it another characteristic result — a certain more or less malicious satisfaction in throwing into as strong relief as possible the great gulf fixed between Philistinism and the elect. That, to be sure, is a by-product, rather than an end sought for its own sake. But it is an almost inevitable concomitant of the sort of reaction which found typical expression in Baudelaire's axiom: *le beau est toujours bizarre.* "Fleurs du Mal" may not have been written expressly *d'étonner le bourgeois,* but neither its author nor any of the *Symbolistes,* nor Oscar Wilde nor any of that circle, put far behind his back the temptation to "shock the middle classes." If the *frisson nouveau,* which was to the elect a delicately titillating shudder, happened to set the teeth of the Philistines chattering in a convulsion, two goodly birds had been killed with the same stone. Now it is obvious that to stress to the limit the element of strangeness in beauty is at the same time to run a line of cleavage sharply through the general community. It is, in other words, to make the enjoyment of poetry primarily an affair of the *illuminati,* or the *cognoscenti,* or whatever other flattering unction we may turn into a name. "The beautiful," declared the Goncourts, "is that which seems abominable to uneducated eyes. The beautiful is that which your mistress or your cook instinctively finds hideous." And that is the inexorable logic of the recoil from the banal to the *outré.*

Let us grant at once that it is the excess of a virtue. But whatever our admission, it remains excess. In its fruitful recognition of the strange as an inherent element of beauty, it overlooks the power, more strong in beauty, born of the familiar. For the greatest art — and by that I mean what the insurgents themselves with virtual unanimity have always admitted as such — the greatest art, from Homer down, has had its roots deep in the common stuff. It may and will have overtones; it may and will awaken thoughts beyond the reaches of the average soul. But no attempt to make poetry once more a vital, civilizing force need ever hope to attain its goal, if it sets to work solely by way of the initiates and the elect. For what the art of the coterie ignores is the weighty fact that the very public which it scouts wants in reality more than it knows it wants. The more or less crude touching of the springs of laughter and of tears, of love, and pity, and indignation, and adventure — this which it thinks is all it asks, is merely the instrument ready at the artist's hand for creating and satisfying finer needs. The Elizabethan public wanted blood and thunder; Shakespeare took the raw materials of melodrama, and gave it "Hamlet." And "Hamlet" still fills the house. That is the case in a nutshell. For the public will accept what the artist has to give, if the artist is big enough and wise enough to build on ground common to the masses and the coterie. The finest and most exquisite art need make no compromise whatever with the public taste. At its height it transcends and transmutes that taste; it responds, and in its response creates. If this be error and upon me proved, then Dante, and Chaucer, and Shakespeare, and Goethe wrote amiss.

There is still another corollary of the individualistic bent of revolt. It is prone to insist on being a law unto itself. Remy de Gourmont characterizes *Symbolisme* as "individualism in literature, liberty of art, abandonment of existing forms. . . . The sole excuse," he continues, "which a man can have for writing is to write down himself, to unveil for others the sort of world which mirrors itself in his individual glass. . . . *He should create his own æsthetics — and we should admit as many æsthetics as there are original minds*, and judge them for what they are and not for what they are not." This is quoted in the Preface to the 1916 "Imagist Anthology," with the remark: "In this sense the Imagists are the descendants of the *Symbolistes;* they are Individualists." And the Preface closes with this temperate and disarming sentence: "We are

young, we are experimentalists, but we ask to
be judged by our own standards, not by those
which have governed other men at other times."
Most heartily, yes! "A whetston is no kerving
instrument," says Pandar, "and yet it maketh
sharpe kerving toles." And it is mere captious-
ness masquerading in the guise of criticism, that
cavils at a whetstone because it's not a sword-
blade, or demands that a sword-blade shall not
flash and cut, but whet. It is the inalienable right
of any movement to insist that its accomplishment be judged in the light of what it has set out
to do, and not as if it were attempting what the
critics might, and probably would, attempt. But
who shall assess the relative values of the ends?
"That is poetry," says Professor Saintsbury,
in a moment of relaxation, "that is poetry to a
man which produces on him such poetical effects
as he is capable of receiving." And, we might
fairly add, that is poetry to a critic which produces on him such poetical effects as he is capable
of perceiving. We seem, in a word, to be con-
fronted with Chaos and old Night, with as many
poetries as there are poets, critics, and lay readers
in the world.

But we are not yet, I think, driven to accept
a poetic Petrograd as our Parnassus. Individual

aims, however successfully attained, fall ulti-
mately into place in a scheme of values. And that
adjustment of values comes about through no
individual critic or group of critics, but through
the relentless judgment of that community of
all the communities which persists undisturbed
through the waves and the billows of each successive generation. Individualism in poetry is
worth having at all hazards. The hazards are
there, but the game is well worth the candle. Yet
we are not thereby called upon to abrogate the
standards of values that are fixed, not by you and
not by me, but by the taciturnity of time.

The peculiar separateness of recent insurgent
movements — to come back for a moment to the
concrete — appears in another and more curious
fact. *Symbolisme* in France during the eighties,
decadence (or what you will) in England in the
nineties, and now the "New Poetry" of the present decade on both sides of the water, have each
been convoyed to immortality by an extremely
active flotilla of little periodicals. In France there
were *L'Hydropathe*, *Le Chat-Noir*, *Lutèce*, the
first and second *Vogue*, *La Revue Indépendent*,
Le Décadent, *La Cravache*, and *Art et Critique;*
in England appeared *The Yellow Book*, *The
Savoy*, *The National Observer*, *The Pageant*, *The*

Dome, and *The New Age.* And now we — a little late in the game, but ignoring with admirable aplomb the fact that we are tardy — we of the current decade have, or have had (for the things are deciduous), *The Egoist, Blast, The Poetry Review, Poetry, Others,* and *The Little Review.* And the last carries, nailed to the mast of its cover, the legend: "A Magazine of the Arts, making no Compromise with the Public Taste." The trumpets of the elect are still blowing about the stubborn walls of Jericho. And indeed I cannot put more tersely the general attitude of the fervid little insurgent periodicals towards the public, than in a superb remark of the equally insurgent Billy Sunday: "They say I rub the fur the wrong way. *I* say, let the cats turn round!"

For myself, I confess to unfeigned delight in the insurgent propaganda. Its fine ardor and alacrity of spirit, its enthusiasm for ideals, its eager hospitality to all poetic Ishmaelites, self-exiled from Abraham's bosom, are metal more attractive than a complacent and impeccably correct inertia. And militant poetry is more to edification than poetic or any other pacifism. "I was ever a fighter, so one fight more," might serve as a motto for many a poet besides Robert

Browning. It is true that the war drums throb
no longer as in the robust anathemas of Ritson,
and Percy, and Warton, when the critics clothed
their necks in thunder, and the poets pawed in
the valley; a slighter breed can scarcely hope to
draw Ulysses' bow. But the electric amenities
that pass between artistic temperaments at different tensions still find free play. And there are
happy moments when the periodicals emulate
the practice of the late author of the "Way of
all Flesh": "I am," some of you will remember
Butler said, "the *enfant terrible* of literature and
science. If I cannot, and I know I cannot, get
the literary and scientific big-wigs to give me a
shilling, I can, and I know I can, heave bricks
into the middle of them." And bricks fly freely
across the embattled slopes of the new Parnassus. Since, however, in the case of poetry insurgent, the critics are apt to be those *bêtes noires*
of the inner circle, "the sterile professors," the
contest is scarcely an even one. But in the main,
the revolutionists in poetry are quite the mild-
est-mannered men that ever scuttled ship, or
cut a throat. And the insurgent journals, from
the eighties on, have busily combined the functions of a gadfly and a star, stinging and beck-
oning with the same facility. Above all, it is to

their ephemeral pages that we must turn, if we seek the harbor from which many a rare spirit has set out for immortality.

I am, however, emphasizing for the moment that type of revolt which leads to the poetry of the coterie. For most of the little periodicals have been, and are, the organs of a group. The milieu from which the *Symboliste* journals sprang is set forth with precision and verve in André Barre's "Le Symbolisme." And their Anglo-Saxon successors owe their idiosyncracies to a not dissimilar environment. But this aspect of revolt is, of course, but a single strand in a mingled yarn. Revolt has, in fact, as many directions as a bursting bomb. The same recoil from accepted themes and formulas that sends one group to the special, exquisite perfume of China or Japan, dispatches another to the stark realism of Chicago or Spoon River. And the divergent tendencies may synchronize or overlap, and the same insurgent journal print poems as antipodal as a slaughter house and a hand-painted fan. For literary movements have a disconcerting habit of complexity, and the common bond between variant and simultaneous avatars of the spirit of revolt is often merely "a general union of total dissent." Moreover, reaction against reaction is one of the most fa-

miliar of all the phenomena of revolt. The preoccupation of poetry with the exquisite and the
remote has more than once set up a sharp recoil
to the nudities and crudities of the sheerest nat-
uralism. Extreme breeds extreme, and in company with fiction and the drama, poetry plunges
like a falling star from the circle of the elect
to bury itself for a time in the contemplation
of characters who, in the words of Mr. Wells,
"crawl along drain pipes till they die." And
then, when it tires (to paraphrase Huysmans)
of the great road so deeply dug out by Zola, it
rises again to trace the parallel pathway in the
air — "now up, now doun, as boket in a welle."

For art behaves uncommonly like the rest of
us:

> . . . I've been three weeks [here] shut within my
>   mew,
> A-painting for the great man, saints and saints
> And saints again . . .
> Ouf! I leaned out of the window for fresh air.
> There came a hurry of feet and little feet . . .
> And a face that looked up . . . zooks, sir, flesh and
>   blood,
> That's all I'm made of! Into shreds it went,
> Curtain and counterpane and coverlet —

and you know the rest. And Fra Lippo Lippi
has had many a follower. "Saints and saints and

saints again," in art and actuality, drive us to sinners, and from sinners we fly back again to saints. There will always be revolt in poetry, so long as action and reaction play their systole and diastole in life.

We are confronting a condition, then, and not a theory. It will not do to say magisterially: "Take the child away!" I suspect that even exhortation is superfluous. Like its forbears, it will burn its own fingers, and go its own gait, and one day awake to the fact that not only has it ceased itself to be revolt, but has become the cause of revolt in others. And poetry should be the last to rebel against the operation of poetic justice. What I should like to write over the door of every stronghold of revolt is the motto over the gateway of the castle in the folk-tale: "Be bold, be bold — but not too bold!" To which the insurgents will promptly and properly retort, with Hamlet, "Be not too *tame*, neither!" And both are right.

V

THE DICTION OF POETRY VERSUS POETIC DICTION

St. Peter admirably enjoins us to be ready always to give an answer to every man that asks us a reason for the faith that is in us, with meekness and fear. And one of the greatest services which the present insurgent movement is performing is in sending us back to first principles, in a salutary endeavor after such preparedness. For it is a strong offensive that is on, and not all the lines are holding. To take stock of resources, accordingly, is more or less incumbent upon all of us.

It is about some of the fundamentals of poetry that the sharpest issues have been raised, and we are bound, I think, to make an effort to reach clearness. And in doing this I propose to abide by the method of procedure we have so far followed. I am not primarily concerned with the present movement *per se*, but rather with the important questions which are being raised once more about poetry itself. It is these larger poetic problems, then, in the light of what is going on to-day, that constitute the subject of the remainder of this volume. And among them the diction of poetry is now, as it has always been, a vigorously mooted point.

Let us take the bull by the horns at once. What is the difference between the diction of poetry and the diction of prose? And by prose I mean now plain, work-a-day prose, not artistic or elevated prose. And I am limiting poetry to poetry in verse. The problem of so-called prose-poetry or poetic prose will concern us later.

The difference, then, between the diction of poetry and that of prose depends on a difference between the functions of words in the two mediums. The business of words in prose is primarily to *state;* in poetry, not only to state, but also (and sometimes primarily) to *suggest.* We may gain clearness by setting over against poetry, for the moment, purely expository, scientific prose. In such prose words may be used for their exact, precisely delimited meaning only, speaking to the hard, clear intellect alone. Any blurring of their sharp definiteness by vague, or especially by emotional associations, intrudes at once a disturbing influence. The terms must be cold as a diagram. That is why the sciences build up their technical terminologies, in which one word conveys one idea, and one idea only, and awakens no more emotion than the binomial theorem. To sum up what I am saying by using myself a technical term, words in scientific prose are used for their *denotation*. They must suggest nothing beyond the rigorous exactitude of their sense.

But in poetry the case is fundamentally different. For poetry, though it speaks to the intellect, is directed equally to the emotions. And that which scientific prose is bent on ruthlessly excising — namely the suggestions, the *connotation* of words — that constitutes in large degree the very stuff with which the poet works. For words stir our feelings, not through a precise delimitation of their sense, but through their enveloping atmosphere of associations. "Not poppy, nor mandragora, Nor all the drowsy syrups of the world" — read that, and the hovering associations merge and blend, and not one word produces its effect through what a dictionary can afford. "We bring the hyacinth-violets, sweet, bare, chill to the touch." That is a bit of Imagist verse, and "violets, sweet, bare, chill to the touch," owes its clear and delicate beauty, not to the lucid exactness of the epithets alone, but even more to a composing of their faint and elusive suggestion into an impression not remotely resembling the fugitive and chilly perfume of the flowers themselves. "In the style of poetry," says Joubert, in one of his luminous "Pensées," "each word reverberates like the note of a well-tuned lyre, and always leaves behind it a multitude of vibrations." For over that which we call the meaning of the words a poet uses, there goes on an incessant play of suggestion, caught from each user's own adventures among words — flashes that come and vanish, stirrings of memories, unfoldings of vistas — and the poet builds up his fabric out of both the basic meanings and the overtones. He does n't create the overtones, any more than he creates the meanings; both are there. What he does create is a harmony. For his exquisite art consists, not in sacrificing either for the other, but in holding the balance true between the two. Verlaine said the thing once for all, in his "Art poétique," when he spoke of "la chanson grise *Où l'Indécis au Précis se joint*." For it is the successful blending of the undefined and the definite in words that constitutes the triumph of the poet's art.

Between purely scientific prose at the one end of the scale, and verse that is saturated with emotion at the other, there are, of course, endless gradations in the balance between the denotation of words and their connotation. But in general, the bare significance of words plays the larger part in prose; their associations, an essential and sometimes a major part in poetry.

Now these facts are constantly put upon wrong inferences, and the conclusion drawn that poetry has a peculiar diction of its own — that "poetic" words, as we call them, must be somehow different from the words of every-day prose. They may be, or they may not be. And the whole question of poetic diction has been confused by isolating it from the fundamental facts of usage. Let us see if the bringing together of a number of these perfectly familiar facts may not conduce to clearness.

Everybody has several vocabularies. Which is merely saying in other words that each of us belongs to a number of communities. We talk in the bosom of our family in a way different from that in which we discourse on state occasions. I permit myself, in speaking to a body of students with whom I have come to stand in fairly close relations, a freedom in the use of colloquialisms which I should not indulge in, were I reading a formal paper before a learned society. The diction of a sermon is not quite that of an after-dinner speech. Nor do people write for the *British Quarterly* exactly as they write for *Punch*. We shift our vocabularies, as we pass from clothes to clothes, and for the same reason. The character of the occasion determines each. Moreover, there is an extensive tract common to all the vocabularies that we possess. We don't talk like a book at one time, and at another discard every word that might adorn the printed page. But we do, on grave or more formal occasions, draw largely on one element of our vocabulary; whereas, in the freedom of intimate circles, when the touch is light, our drafts are on an entirely different fund. Given the same subject-matter, and there are words which we are apt to use on this occasion, others on that; but there is a far larger residuum which we use on all. This is common experience, and needs no argument.

But it helps us, I think, towards a clearer understanding of our immediate problem. For the diction of poetry and the diction of prose have also a vast tract in common. And that common store of words is the backbone of poetry. There are also, of course, words which are proper in prose, but which would be more or less out of place in poetry. There are words which are fitting in verse, that would strike a jarring note in prose. And we shall have to consider the relation to poetry of both these outlying districts of the general vocabulary. But it is the great central tract of diction that is common to both poetry and prose which must claim our attention first.

The very greatest effects of poetry are often produced without the use of a single word which might not be employed in ordinary speech. What words in the following passages are not, *as words*, equally at home in prose?

> And all our yesterdays have lighted fools
> The way to dusty death. Out, out, brief candle!
> Life's but a walking shadow, a poor player
> That struts and frets his hour upon the stage,
> And then is heard no more.

> Fear no more the heat o' the sun,
>   Nor the furious winter's rages.

> Brightness falls from the air;
> Queens have died young and fair.

> Had we never lov'd sae kindly,
> Had we never lov'd sae blindly,
> Never met — or never parted,
> We had ne'er been broken-hearted.

> But where the dead leaf fell, there did it rest.

> And never lifted up a single stone.

Poetry may be poetry, then, and the loftiest at that, without employing the diction which we call poetic. Its richest store lies within and not without the tract that it holds in common with prose. And our original question may now receive a fuller answer.

The fundamental difference between poetry and prose, so far as their diction is concerned, is not in the words themselves, but in the use that is made of the words. Poetry communicates ideas, but it does more. It is concerned with truth "carried alive into the heart by passion"; it aims at the transmission, through the exercise of imaginative energy, of impressions, not facts; and its words take up and absorb fresh potencies from these powerful elements in which they move. They are the same words precisely as when they occur in prose. But a new virtue (in the fine old sense of the term) has passed into them. It is not merely that their meaning is determined by their context. It is both that and more. To a certain degree in prose and essentially in poetry, words are impregnated by their context; they are subdued to what they work in, like the dyer's hand. To put the same thing barely, words have an emotional and imaginative, as well as an intellectual context. The last is the chief determining factor in prose; it is the first which is powerfully operative in poetry.

Let us return for a moment, with this in mind, to one or two of the passages already quoted Here is the tenth line of "Hyperion": "But where the dead leaf fell, there did it rest." That has been referred to (and I think justly) as "a line almost as intense and full of the essence of poetry as any line in our language." Why? Certainly not on account of any independent poetical quality in a single one of its ten un-impassioned and familiar monosyllables. It is something else. What the line does is to resume and gather up in one penetratingly simple de-tail, the whole of that motionless, hueless, silent landscape on which we have already dwelt; and it is the imaginative intensity of the whole con-ception which transforms every syllable of its closing line. So Wordsworth's: "And never lifted up a single stone," focuses in itself the stark simplicity of the rustic tragedy of "Michael." And it is the same power of imbuing with poignant emotional suggestion words which are without distinction in themselves that finds su-preme expression, times without number, in Dante; as in the famous: "Quel giorno più non vi leggemmo avante" — "That day they read in it no farther." Indeed, it is very largely through just this penetration of familiar words with imaginative quality that poetry exercises its creative energy.

> Brightness *falls* from the air.

> That time of year thou mayst in me behold
> When yellow leaves, or none, or few, do *hang*
> Upon those boughs which *shake* against the cold.

"Falls," "hang," and "shake" mean what they mean in prose; but there has been exerted on them an influence which, without distorting or in any way infringing on their ordinary sense, has endowed them with the power to stir imagination in us.

Is it possible, now, to set any limit to this transfusing power which poetry exercises over words? Are there, to put it differently, words which remain intractable to its assimilating influence? It is perilous to make categorical assertions. If the imaginative energy is strong enough, almost no word can remain insoluble, and a flat denial of poetic possibilities, in the case of any vocable, is liable to disastrous refutation by a triumphant instance of the "poetizing' (as Goldsmith calls it) of that very word. "Intrinsicate" is a word we should rule out at once on general principles. And there it stands, superb in its resolution of Cleopatra's trenchant monosyllables:

> Come, thou mortal wretch,
> With thy sharp teeth this knot *intrinsicate*
> Of life at once untie.

"Vitreous" is a prose word, if ever there was one. Yet, listen!

> Smile O voluptuous cool-breath'd earth!
> Earth of the slumbering and liquid trees!
> Earth of departed sunset — earth of the mountains misty-topt!
> Earth of the *vitreous* pour of the full moon just tinged with blue!
> Far-swooping elbow'd earth — rich apple-blossom'd earth!
> Smile, for your lover comes.

It would take a word of tougher fibre than even "vitreous," to withstand the amalgamating power of such a context as that! And we might illustrate endlessly. There are misguided souls who think that a word like "scratch," for example, is unpoetic. In splendid isolation, I suppose it is. But in poetry that is worthy of the name there are no isolated words. Their suggestions interpenetrate each other, and every word, even "scratch," may take on, chameleon-like, the colors of its fellows:

Then a mile of warm sea-scented beach;
Three fields to cross till a farm appears;
A tap at the pane, the quick sharp *scratch*
And blue spurt of a lighted match,
And a voice less loud, through its joys and fears,
Than the two hearts beating each to each.

If the current runs strong, there are few words which it cannot safely carry with it.

It is when the stream runs shallow, that the words refuse to blend. They jut out from their context, unassimilated entities. I have just used the figure of a stream. Here is a quatrain quoted with gusto by Professor Everett of beloved memory, in "Poetry, Comedy, and Duty":

The essence of mind's being is the stream of thought,
  Difference of mind's being is difference of the stream;
Within this single difference may be brought
  The countless differences that are or seem.

Nothing is wrong with the *words*, so far as their poetic potentialities are concerned. "Difference" is a bit over-worked, to be sure, but it is poetically sound:

But she is in her grave, and, oh,
  The *difference* to me!

"Essence" is unimpeachable:

His glassy *essence*, like an angry ape,
Plays such fantastic tricks before high heaven
As make the angels weep.

And the other words need no bush. One thing only is the matter with the quatrain. It is n't poetry at all. It is innocent of the slightest trace of imaginative fusion. No stream whatever pulses through it. And the words remain words — not winged things, with "colors dipt in heaven."

Set beside this another treatment of a similar theme, this time by a philosopher who was a poet too:

> Thy summer voice, Musketaquit,
> Repeats the music of the rain;
> But sweeter rivers pulsing flit
> Through thee, as thou through Concord Plain.
>
> Thou in thy narrow banks art pent:
> The stream I love unbounded goes
> Through flood and sea and firmament;
> Through light, through life, it forward flows.
>
> I see the *inundation* sweet,
> I hear the spending of the stream
> Through years, through men, through nature fleet,
> Through love and thought, through power
>   and dream.
>
> Musketaquit, a goblin strong,
> Of shard and flint makes jewels gay;
> They lose their grief who hear his song,
> And where he winds is the day of day.
>
> So forth and brighter fares my stream, —
> Who drink it shall not thirst again;
> No darkness stains its equal gleam,
> And ages drop in it like rain.

"Inundation," if you please, is less poetic (as we say) than either "difference" or "essence." But true poetry, like Musketaquit, makes jewels out of shards and flints.

Words in themselves, then, are neither poetic nor unpoetic. They become poetic, or they remain unassimilated prose, according as the poet's imaginative energy is or is not sufficiently powerful to absorb them.

If there are words which may become poetic, are there words which are inherently poetical to start with? Let us begin with an assumption that may be safely made. There are, without question, words which are more readily assimilated by poetry than others, and these are, for the most part, words which are associated with *objects* that stir the sort of emotion which is the basis of poetry — with the immemorial, universal phenomena of soul and sense, which are common ground for all humanity. Sun, moon, and stars, the sea, the fall of evening, night and sleep, the fireside, roads, sounds innumerable (as of footsteps, the rain, running water, winds, the surf, sheep-bells, bird notes, flutes), certain odors and colors, the seasons, birth and especially death, and all the throng of emotional experiences that come between them, together with all the familiar homely objects of daily use — it is needless more than to suggest. That which gives to Hebrew poetry, for instance, its depth and poignancy is just this elemental quality in its words. The large and simple and permanent objects and elements of life — the eternal hills, the treasures of the snow, rain coming down upon mown grass, winds and all weathers, the rock in the desert, still water in pasture lands and the sea that roars and is troubled, sleep and the fleetingness of dreams, the mystery of birth and death — all the perennial, elemental processes of nature, all the changing, yet abiding physiognomy of earth and sky, were charged for psalmist and prophet with spiritual significance, and woven into the very texture of their speech.

And a man shall be as an hiding place from the wind, and a covert from the tempest; as rivers of water in a dry place, as the shadow of a great rock in a weary land; Thy righteousness is like the great mountains; thy judgments are a great deep; He shall come down like rain upon the mown grass: as showers that water the earth; Thou carriest them away as with a flood; they are as a sleep; As a dream when one awaketh; so, O Lord . . . thou shalt despise their image; As for man, his days are as grass; as a flower of the field, so he flourisheth; for the wind passeth over it, and it is gone; and the place thereof shall know it no more.

Utter simplicity, limpid clearness, the vividness

of direct, authentic vision of "unworded things
and old": these are the salient qualities of the
diction of the poetry of the Bible. I may not at
the moment speak of the influence of the King
James version upon the diction of English
poetry. What I am concerned with now is the
readiness for poetic use of words which, like
those of Hebrew poetry, are pervaded already
with emotional or imaginative suggestion. Here
are two lines from Stevenson's "Requiem":

> Home is the sailor, home from sea,
> And the hunter home from the hill.

The words themselves are latent poetry —
which is a very different thing from saying that
they are poetic diction.

"Home," "sailor," "sea," "hunter," and
"hill," then, are not poetic, any more than they
are prose words. They are both. They simply
happen to belong to that element of the common
vocabulary which is especially apt for the poet's
use. And out of this arises a common fallacy.
For all five words that I have named are of native origin, as, indeed, are most of the words which
come closest to men's business and bosoms. And
the statement is not infrequently made that
Saxon words are more "poetic" than the words

of foreign, chiefly Latin origin, in which our con-
glomerate speech abounds. There is just so much
of truth in that as lies in the fact that the native
stock is peculiarly endowed with homely vigor,
and forthrightness, and vividness, and concrete-
ness, all of which are qualities of worth in poetry.
But other words than native words possess these
qualities, and they are not the only qualities of
poetry. For poetry is protean in its moods and
dispositions, and its diction changes with its
bents and its occasions, as yours does or mine.
And absolutely the only test of the poetic
quality of a word is its ability to hold its own
triumphantly in its particular poetic setting.

I suspect that the greatest poetry *is*, as a rule,
what Fitzgerald calls "a concise and simple way
of saying great things." But all poets are not
concise and simple souls, and even the simplest
souls have complex moments. Moreover, the potential of poetry, so to speak, shifts incessantly,
from the most impassioned lyric to the coldest,
keenest satire. Not even a poet can live perpetually at white heat without burning out. And
certainly no sane reader of poetry cares to glow
with emotion as a steady regimen. Poe's doctrine of brevity, as a mandate laid upon poetry
by the inflexible nature of things, is sound, in

so far as it rests on the indisputable fact that we
cannot feel intensely at too long a stretch without something snapping or sinking limp. Shakespeare knew what he was doing, when he sent the
drunken porter stumbling across the stage just
when he did. In other words, poetry is not always
tugging at our heartstrings. It sweeps the chords
of all the faculties that we possess. When it is
forthright, it deals in forthright words; when
thought plays glancing and shifting above the
deeper current, its diction becomes prismatic and
subtle with intellectual quality; when it runs
through the whole gamut, then, as Coleridge has
it, "words that convey feelings, and words that
flash images, and words of abstract notion, flow
together, and . . . rush on like a stream."

Saxon words, then, are no more inherently
poetic than the naturalized aliens of our richly
cosmopolitan tongue. They fit more poetic occasions, as is inevitable, and that is all.

> Break, break, break,
>   On thy cold gray stones, O Sea!
> And I would that my tongue could utter
>   The thoughts that arise in me —

has not a single word that is n't native Saxon
(and only two that are n't monosyllables), and it
owes its poignancy largely to that fact. But,

> When to the sessions of sweet silent thought
> I summon up remembrance of things past —

owes its certainly no less exquisite poetic quality to five words — "sessions," "silent," "summon," "remembrance," "past" — which are of Latin origin. And he would be rash, indeed, who should say that one word was more poetic than another in passages like these, where it is the consummate balance of native and foreign-born, monosyllable and polysyllable, that achieves the miracle:

> Magic casements, opening on the foam
> Of perilous seas, in faëry lands forlorn.

> Along the cool sequester'd vale of life
> They kept the noiseless tenor of their way.

> What is excellent,
> As God lives, is permanent;
> Hearts are dust, hearts' loves remain.

The miracle can be achieved, to be sure, by bare monosyllables alone:

> Since there's no help, come, let us kiss and part!
> Nay, I have done; you get no more of me!
> And I am glad, yea, glad with all my heart,
> That thus so cleanly I myself can free.

There are thirty-three monosyllables in succession, and in all four lines but two words that are not. But,

> The multitudinous seas incarnadine,

with its roll of sonorous Latin polysyllables; and

> Splits the unwedgeable and gnarled oak,

with its tough and massy native polysyllables; and

> In the dark backward and abysm of time,

with its poising of one against the other, are all the essence of poetry. And so is that other line without a single polysyllable with which to bless itself:

> But where the dead leaf fell, there did it rest.

There is, accordingly, no law whatever that can be laid down, whereby one word is taken and another left by poetry at large. This or that particular poem has a circumscribed range of choice, determined by its own unity of impression. *Poems* are inevitably limited; *poetry* is not. And what is "Don Juan's" meat may be "The Excursion's" poison. Here is a sample:

> All these things will be specified in time,
>   With strict regard to Aristotle's rules,
> The *Vade Mecum* of the true sublime,
>   Which makes so many poets, and some fools:
> Prose poets like blank-verse, I'm fond of ryme,
>   Good workmen never quarrel with their tools;
> I've got new mythological machinery,
> And very handsome supernatural scenery.

Imagine any single word of that in the "Ode to the West Wind" or "La Belle Dame Sans Merci"! There are, I know, ethereal spirits who deny that "Don Juan" is poetry. From such I must gently but firmly part company. A fugitive and cloistered poetry that never at any time heard the chimes at midnight, is ill-accommodated to the uses of this world. "Dost thou think, because [Milton, and Southey, and Wordsworth are verbally] virtuous, there shall be no more cakes and ale? Yes, by Saint Anne, and ginger shall be hot i' the mouth too," for Chaucer, and Burns, and Byron. And they will by no means always employ "a stately speech, Such as grave Livers do in Scotland use, Religious men, who give to God and man their dues." Moreover, if poetry chooses to discourse in slippered ease, it may fall into colloquialisms with the best of us:

> Shut, shut the door, good John! fatigu'd, I said,
> Tie up the knocker, say I'm sick, I'm dead.
> The Dog-star rages! nay 't is past a doubt,
> All Bedlam, or Parnassus, is let out . . .
> A dire dilemma! either way I'm sped,
> If foes, they write, if friends, they read me dead . . .
> All my demurs but double his attacks;
> At last he whispers, "Do; and we go snacks."

The diction of poetry includes every word which poetry can use.

There are, however, two classes of words about which the battle has always raged, as it rages now, with particular intensity — antiquated and brand-new words; or, more exactly, archaisms and neologisms. And first as regards archaisms.

Gray, in one of his letters, makes the following statement: "As to matter of style, I have this to say: The language of the age is never the language of poetry; except among the French, whose verse, where the thought or image does not support it, differs in nothing from prose. Our poetry, on the contrary, has a language peculiar to itself." I have been running counter to that very high authority, in respect to the latter statement, although the difference is far more a question of interpretation than of fact. What of the other dictum: "The language of the age is never the language of poetry"? As a matter of fact, independently of all theory, it is true. Poetry, law, ecclesiastical ritual, and sports are the four most powerful conservators, not only of older words, but also of older forms of words, and older meanings. And in all four cases this tenaciousness is due to the strong traditional character of their usages. The one point which I wish to emphasize is this: archaic words are as proper to poetry as any other words. The only question that we have a right to raise, is that of their fitness to their particular use. They are no more specifically poetic, except in so far as they may carry richer associations, than the current coin of speech. "Words borrowed of antiquity," says Ben Jonson, in those observations on style in the "Discoveries," whose every rift is packed with ore, "do lend a kind of majesty to style; . . . for they have the authority of years, and out of their intermission do win themselves a kind of gracelike newness." On the other hand, archaic words may even be less poetically effective — as they certainly are, when they are intruded for their own sake, or under a mistaken notion of their sanctity. There are words which vie with Cleopatra living: "Age cannot wither them, nor custom stale Their infinite variety." There are words which are like Cleopatra dead: "Now she is very old and dry and faded, With black bitumen they have sealed up her mouth." It is the poet's instinct that must determine which is which.

Spenser, of course, is the most notorious example of over-indulgence in an archaic diction, and many of you are familiar with the justification of his practice in the Epistle Dedicatory to the "Shepheardes Calender." I shall quote but one of

E. K.'s sentences: "In my opinion it is one spec-
ail prayse of many, whych are dew to this Poete,
that he hath laboured to restore, as to theyr
rightfull heritage, such good and naturall English
words, as have ben long time out of use, and
almost cleane disherited." Against that, however, we must set Ben Jonson's terse remark:
"Spenser, in affecting the ancients, writ no language." As usual, the whole truth lies neither
with the poet nor with his critics. Dryden brings
his stalwart common sense to bear upon the
problem, and clarifies the issue: "If the first end
of a writer be to be understood, then, as his
language grows obsolete, his thoughts must
grow obscure. . . . When an ancient word, for its
sound and significancy, deserves to be revived,
I have that reasonable veneration for antiquity
to restore it. All beyond this is superstition."

And so we are brought back to our fundamental principle of intelligibility. And the
charge of unintelligibility sometimes laid at the
door of archaisms is not always a man of straw.
Wordsworth's poem entitled "The Force of
Prayer" begins as follows: "What is good for a
bootless bene?" And this is what Lamb wrote to
Wordsworth: "Apropos — when I first opened
upon the just-mentioned poem, in a careless tone,

I said to Mary, as if putting a riddle, '*What is good for a bootless bene?*' To which with infinite presence of mind, she answered, 'A shoeless pea.' It was the first joke she ever made." Lamb proceeds, it must be added, to apologize for his levity on such an occasion, but I fear it was warranted. Wordsworth, to be sure, condescends to our weakness in the premises, for the poem at once becomes a glossary:

> " What is good for a bootless bene?"
> With these dark words begins my Tale;
> *And their meaning is*, whence can comfort spring
> When Prayer is of no avail?

But all archaisers are not so thoughtful!

Quite apart from intelligibility, however, the congruity of the diction with the tone and spirit of the individual poem constitutes the determining factor. Archaisms are of the very substance of "The Ancient Mariner," and "The Blessed Damozel"; they would strike a hopelessly jarring note in "Bishop Blougram's Apology," or the "Barrack Room Ballads." If an archaic word is intelligible, and produces the effect which the poet wishes to produce, it is good poetic gold. On the other hand, Imagist poetry, for example, is right in veering away from any tinge of archaism in its diction, because it is aiming at an effect with which such diction is inconsistent. One may question, if one please, the worth of the effect; that, for the moment, is another question. Once grant the aim of the modernists, however, and their instinct in this respect is sound. Both in his acceptances and his rejections of words, then, the burden of proof rests on the poet. And the proof even of his pudding is the eating of it.

Precisely the same principles of intelligibility and fitness apply to the use of neologisms in poetry. There goes on in any living language an incessant streaming up into good and accepted usage of low words, new words, strange words, technical words. Terms of the utmost dignity to-day began as slang, and a word that is slang to-day may be President (so to speak) to-morrow. Scientific inventions crowd into every nook and cranny of our lives, and scraps of the terminology of science follow them. War heaves up into the level stretches of our every-day, civilian speech masses of words, a few months ago unknown, but now glib on our tongues. There are always new words, and there always will be, so long as the language lives, and they are often fresh and vivid as well as new. Must poetry keep hands off? Well, that depends upon just two things: what the poet is trying to achieve; and what he is willing to risk. If that which he is writing demands the use of Dante's "sieve for noble words," the newcomers will undoubtedly sift through; their patent of nobility is not yet conferred. If, on the other hand, he is writing racily, or colloquially, or in lighter vein, they may fit into his pattern. But in any case, he takes his chances. If they remain at par or advance, he wins; if they depreciate, his margin of safety is wiped out. And there, I suppose, lies one of the sweet uses of revolt. Your insurgent is adventurous, and takes the chances. He proposes the new word (I am quoting Dryden) to be naturalized, by using it himself; "and, if the public approves of it, the bill passes." As Meredith declares, "poetic rashness of the right quality enriches the language." But (still to allow the poets themselves to speak of what they know) Ben Jonson shows the more excellent way. For "the eldest of the present, and the newest of the past language, is the best."

So much for general principles. Let us see, now, what happens when poetry labors under the delusion that, to be poetic, it must get away from the basic elements of the general vocabulary to a peculiar diction of its own. I shall use the vagaries of the eighteenth century to point my implicit moral, and shall follow briefly the vicissitudes of poetic diction down to the present active propaganda against it. And obviously suggestion rather than exhaustiveness must be my aim.

What led to the outbreak of a diction that swept over the eighteenth century like the plague, is of the utmost interest, but impossible of treatment here. I must plunge *in medias res*. And I shall have to hold up Pope himself as a terrible example. Since that is so, I wish to say explicitly that Pope, in the bulk of his work, is absolute master of the raciest, most familiar, most cogent and telling elements of the vernacular, and one of the most consummate craftsmen who ever dealt in words. If he, like his Erasmus, is a "great injur'd name," it is largely because his imitators perpetuated his worst, which was within their scope, and not his best, which was beyond their reach. The tendency, then, of which Pope was at the same time a result and an active cause, was, for one thing, away from the direct, simple, downright calling of things by their names, if the things were regarded as in any way common or unclean. To call a spade a spade was like presenting one's self in company *in puris naturalibus*. It is all very suggestive of Bottom and Snout and the Lion in the "Midsummer Night's Dream." "To bring in a lion," says Bottom, "to bring in — God shield us! — a lion among ladies, is a most dreadful thing; for there is not a more fearful wild-fowl than your lion living." "Therefore," says Snout, "another prologue must tell he is not a lion." And so, for the benefit of artistic sensibilities, in the poetry we are considering, the lions roar as gently as any sucking dove. The wind is softened to "the trembling zephyr," or "the fragrant gale." Shakespeare's "rude, imperious surge" becomes "the sprightly flood," or "swelling tide"; a boot is "the shining leather that encased the limb"; a pipe is "the short tube that fumes beneath the nose"; negroes are "Afric's sable progeny"; bulls are "monarchs of the brindled breed"; pigs, "the grunting, bristly kind"; sheep, "the soft, fearful people." Does one make coffee? "From silver spouts the grateful liquors glide, While China's earth receives the smoking tide." Does one serve fish and fowl? "From Darkin's roosts the feathered victims bleed, And Thames still wafts me ocean's scaly breed." Are you blind of one eye? "To one the fates the visual ray deny."

"Ææa's isle," in Keats, "was wondering at the moon." Francis Fawkes wonders too; *he* wonders

"Why silver Phœbe, meek-ey'd queen of night,
Now slackens, now precipitates her flight." And
I wonder with what amazing circumlocution
Fawkes would have said, "Since there's no help,
come, let us kiss and part!"

And I indulge in that remark advisedly. For it
is in the attempts of the eighteenth century to
translate into its own lingo the noble simplicity
of great speech, that poetic diction finds its *re-
ductio ad absurdum*. Francis Fawkes was nobody.
But it's the nobodies of poetry, even to-day, who
are the straws that show the way the wind is
blowing. I wish space permitted me to set down
in antiphonal sequence the twelfth chapter of
Ecclesiastes, and Fawkes's poetizing of it. Here,
however, is a taste of his quality, from his ren-
dering of David's lament over Jonathan:

> Thy love to me was wonderful, passing the love of
> women.

> Thy love was wondrous, soothing all my care,
> *Passing the fond affection of the fair.*

If ever the beauty of Israel was slain upon its
high places, it was then! Let us pass to the
stately lines of the Song of Deborah:

> He asked for water, and she gave him milk; she
> brought forth butter in a lordly dish.

But that is prose; here is poetic diction:

> He ask'd refreshment from the limpid wave,
> The milky beverage to the chief she gave.

Even periphrasis, apparently, could not lift butter to the plane of poetry, and it remains unwept, unhonored, and unsung. But, you will say, it is as patently disingenuous to single out Francis Fawkes, as it would be to pitch upon the veriest camp-follower of the New Poetry as the abstract and brief chronicle of its procedure. Very good. Let us move above the salt. And now I *shall* set down, in antiphonal sequence, a few verses of Isaiah, and Alexander Pope:

> The glory of Lebanon shall be given unto it, the excellency of Carmel and Sharon.

> See lofty Lebanon his head advance,
> See nodding forests on the mountains dance:
> See spicy clouds from lowly Saron rise,
> And Carmel's flow'ry top perfumes the skies!

> Then the eyes of the blind shall be opened, and the ears of the deaf shall be unstopped.

> He from thick films shall purge the visual ray,
> And on the sightless eye-ball pour the day:
> 'T is he th' obstructed paths of sounds shall clear,
> And bid new music charm th' unfolding ear.

> The sun shall be no more thy light by day; neither for brightness shall the moon give light unto thee.

> No more the rising Sun shall gild the morn,
> Nor ev'ning Cynthia fill her silver horn.

Chaucer in wig and small-clothes is too mourn-
ful a spectacle for us to linger over, when instead
of "glad[ing] every flour with his warmnesse,"
his Phœbus now "glads the glebe and paints the
flowery fields"; and I pass on to Homer.

Thus spake she wailing, and stirred unending moan.
Then thirdly Helen led their sore lament.

And now Pope:

Thus spoke the dame, and melted into tears.
Sad Helen next in pomp of grief appears;
Fast from the shining sluices of her eyes
Fall the round crystal drops, while thus she cries.

Some of you will recall the passage in Boswell
which tells of the inextinguishable laughter at Sir
Joshua Reynolds's, one night, when Dr. Grainger read from his manuscript of "The Sugar-
Cane" the line: "Now, Muse, let's sing of *rats*";
and how somebody, slyly looking over the reader's shoulder, saw that the word had been origi-
nally *mice*, but had been altered to *rats*, as more
dignified; and how, finally, the unlucky Grainger
triumphantly substituted for his rats: "the
whisker'd vermin race." I shall make but one
more excerpt from Pope's Homer, in which Pope
makes a similar excursion round Robin Hood's
barn. Here is Homer, in Andrew Lang's prose:

And as when a lazy *ass* going past a field hath the

better of the boys with him, an ass that hath had many
a cudgel broken about his sides, and he fareth into the
deep crop, and wasteth it, while the boys smite him with
cudgels —

and so on. But Pope balks at "ass":

> As *the slow beast, with heavy strength endued,*
> In some wide field by troops of boys pursued,
> Though round his sides a wooden tempest rain,
> Crops the tall harvest, and lays waste the plain;
> Thick on his hide the hollow blows resound,
> *The patient animal* maintains his ground.

Pope justifies himself on the ground that "a
translator owes so much to the taste of the age in
which he lives as not to make too great a compliment to the former [age]; and this induced me to
omit the mention of the word *ass* in the translation." May I give, in its full context, a passage
from one who was not induced to omit the mention of the word *ass?*

> Come, thou mortal wretch,
> With thy sharp teeth this knot intrinsicate
> Of life at once untie. Poor venomous fool,
> Be angry, and despatch. O, couldst thou speak,
> That I might hear thee call great Cæsar *ass*
> Unpolicied!
>   *Char.* O eastern star!
>   *Cleo.*   Peace, peace!
> Dost thou not see my baby at my breast,
> That sucks the nurse asleep?
>   *Char.*   O, break! O, break!
>   *Cleo.* As sweet as balm, as soft as air, as
>   gentle, — O Antony!

If there be such a thing on earth as the grand style, it is that speech, of which *ass* is an integral part. And it passes without break of a line or a jarring syllable into poetry of the most poignant and supernal beauty. And in the juxtaposition of a conventional poetic diction with that supreme embodiment of the diction of poetry, I have made the only comment that I care to make on the merits of the case.

We have already seen that action and reaction are pretty certain to be equal. And everybody knows how Wordsworth reacted against the eighteenth-century poetic diction. The sternest compression and excision are imperative, but I shall try not to be unfair. Wordsworth's doctrine is a compound of fundamental truths and subtle fallacies. And when he wrote with his eye on his theory, and not on the object, the truths slipped out from under him, and the fallacies rode him like hags. When he threw his theory to the winds, "held the hye wey, and lat his gost him lede," he could write like the Angel of the Vision. Now the gist of his theory, as elucidated in the Preface to the "Lyrical Ballads," is this. Poetry should choose incidents and situations from common, preferably humble and rustic life; and it should employ, in relating and describing them,

"*a selection of language really used by men.*" The
reasons for the tenets were, in part, quite wrong,
but the tenets themselves represent a sound and
healthy revolt against an affected and citified
diction, in which the sun never rose across open
fields, but "Sol thro' white curtains shot a
tim'rous ray." In his recoil from the stilted,
however, Wordsworth pitched headlong into the
trivial, and in its rebellion against the artificially
poetic, his diction became the apotheosis of the
prosaic.

> "Now, little Edward, say why so:
>   My little Edward, tell me why." —
> "I cannot tell, I do not know." —
> "Why, this is strange," said I . . .
>
>   At this, my boy hung down his head,
>   He blushed with shame, nor made reply;
>   And three times to the child I said,
> "Why, Edward, tell me why?"
>
>   His head he raised — there was in sight,
>   It caught his eye, he saw it plain —
>   Upon the house-top, glittering bright,
>   A broad and gilded vane.

All the words in these famous stanzas from the
"Anecdote for Fathers" are susceptible of poetic
quality, but there is nothing present to infuse
them with it. And having the form of poetry

without the power thereof, they sink below the
level of prose itself to the prosaic.

> Why bustle thus about your door,
> What means this bustle, Betty Foy?
> Why are you in this mighty fret?
> And why on horseback have you set
> Him whom you love, your Idiot Boy?

Wordsworth wrote to one of the critics of "The
Idiot Boy" a letter which occupies eight full
pages of the "Memoir." Two sentences are of
special interest: "It is probable that the principal
cause of your dislike to this particular poem lies
in the *word* Idiot. If there had been any such
word in our language, *to which we had attacheu
passion*, as lack-wit, half-wit, witless, etc., I
should certainly have employed it in preference;
but there is no such word." The difficulty, however, lies in no single word — certainly not in
"idiot." As Sir Walter Raleigh has said, poets
"redeem words from degradation by a single
noble employment," and Shakespeare had saved
"idiot," if it required salvation:

> . . . It is a tale
> Told by an *idiot*, full of sound and fury,
> Signifying nothing.

The head and front of Wordsworth's offending,
in this and in the other poems of its kind, hath

this extent, no more: *his employment of his words is not noble.* The indictment lies, not against his diction, but against its use. And that use is not infrequently due to a defective sense of humor — a perilous lack, when one is dealing with the potential incongruities that lurk, malignly expectant, in the associations of words. "I never wrote anything with so much glee," said Wordsworth of "The Idiot Boy." It is precisely when Wordsworth is most gleeful that he is most afflicting, for then his touch on words is never sure. And that means Peter Bell, and Betty Foy, and Goody Blake, and Harry Gill, and little Edward, and the Blind Highland Boy who went to sea, not in a bowl, but in

> A household tub, like one of those
> Which women use to wash their clothes.

And Wordsworth's sense of values remained defective, when, flying from Scylla to Charybdis, he changed the tub to a turtle-shell —

> A shell of ample size, and light
> As the pearly car of Amphitrite,
> That sportive dolphins drew.

And yet Wordsworth's theory, stripped of the limitations which he imposed upon it, was absolutely sound. The diction of poetry was to be "a *selection* of language really used by men."

Rightly understood, that means a selection of
the language really used by William Wordsworth, and not of that employed by Betty Foy.
The poet is more than the mouth-piece of an idiot
and his mother. He is the translator of their halt-
ing speech, not a mere emulator of their inartic-
ulateness. Wordsworth says of Michael: "His
mind was keen, Intense, and frugal, apt for all
affairs." That is a selection of the language
really used by men. But it has behind it the
copious stores of Wordsworth's own vocabulary,
from which are culled the apt, and fitting, and
exact words to express a man who could not possibly thus express himself. And a phrase like "keen,
intense, and frugal, apt for all affairs," refutes
once for all the absurdities of "Now, little Edward, say why so." There is a simplicity of diction which reflects a meagre and barren stock;
there is also a simplicity which results from the
winnowing of a rich abundance. The one is
the simplicity of the "Anecdote for Fathers";
the other of "Michael." And in the Tintern
Abbey lines, and the "Ode on the Intimations
of Immortality," and the great sonnets, and in
such lines as:

Whose dwelling is the light of setting suns.

The Winds come to me from the fields of sleep.

And the most ancient heavens, through Thee, are
        fresh and strong.

                . . . to send
Its own deep quiet to restore our hearts.

                . . . old, unhappy, far-off things,
And battles long ago —

in all these, Wordsworth transcends, without
contravening, his theory. He employs the language really used by men, but his employment is
now noble with a nobility attained only by the
greatest. .

The pendulum, however, is always swinging,
and the Romanticists opened up new and vast
regions for poetry. And since they all had, to a
greater or less degree, that *Hang zum Unbe-
grenzten* — that *penchant* for the infinite —
which Goethe ascribed to Byron in particular,
the vocabulary of poetry increased enormously
its store of words of heightened emotional associations, of vague splendors, of richly sensuous
suggestion. The diction of poetry became, with
notable exceptions, opulent, sumptuous, lavish,
rather than pointed, terse, concrete. And this
very opulence of the Romantic diction — at its
best, one of the glories of English poetry —
tended to confuse the issue for the Romanticists'

successors. Words once nobly used were taken to be inherently noble, and were employed to confer on poetry the nobility which it is poetry's function to confer on words. Once more, as so often, words came to be regarded as having in themselves poetic virtue, so that one need only arrange in ordered sequence the proper number of poetic terms, in order to achieve a poem. I am not now speaking primarily of the masters. They usually thought straight amid their splendors. It was when the splendors cut loose from the architectonic compulsion of ideas, and walked off, alone and invertebrate, that poetry became, as practiced by its minor acolytes, the haunt of slumberous glooms, and verdurous gleams, and murmurous darks and deeps. And so there arose a new conventional diction, less crass, but more insidious than that of the eighteenth century — a diction which conferred plenary absolution from the pains of thought upon poet and reader alike. As usual, a powerful poetic force set the echoes reverberating through the pages of minor poetry.

And now against that, in turn, the inevitable reaction has set in. It finds its most sharply defined expression in the principles and practices of the Imagists, to whom, however, it is by no means confined. They merely happen to be the most articulate among the groups. And their tenets are both negative and positive.

Stevenson once wrote to Henry James:

> My two aims may be described as:
> *1st*. War to the adjective.
> *2d*. Death to the optic nerve.

Well, the two battle cries of the New Poetry, as I catch their echoes, are:

1st. War on the eloquent.

2d. Death to the *cliché*.

"Take eloquence and wring its neck," wrote Verlaine in his "Art poétique." That might well be the motto of the present movement, so far as diction is concerned — that, and "A *cliché* is worse than a crime." And the time was undoubtedly ripe for just such a revolt. The pruning-hook was needed, and though it is often used by dreadfully inexpert and ruthless hands, the stock is strong enough to stand it, and to grow the more vigorously for the lopping. The destructive trend of the reaction is of course extreme, but revolutionary movements always are extreme, and the inevitable counter-offensive will win back whatever territory of value is for the moment lost. We may imperturbably possess our souls: "Nothing is here for tears, nothing to wail Or knock the breast." The tide is at a turning; that is all.

But the movement is positive, too, in its attitude towards the diction of poetry. It proposes to use, in the words of the Imagist pronouncement, "the language of common speech, but to employ always the *exact* word, not the nearly-exact, nor the merely decorative word." That is not far from the Kingdom of God, if so be that William Wordsworth is that Kingdom's prophet! It took the pendulum exactly one hundred and fifteen years to swing from Wordsworth's "selection of the language really used by men," out through the interstellar spaces of the Romanticists and the Victorians, and back again to the Imagists' "language of common speech." The *differentia* of the new statement, however, lies in the phrase "to employ always the *exact* word." That has been authoritatively interpreted as meaning "the exact word which conveys the writer's *impression* to the reader." And unless everything that has been said in the opening chapter of this book is wrong, that is sound doctrine.

For poetry gives, not facts, but the poet's impression of facts, and these impressions may and must be of infinite variety. The doctrine of the exact word, so understood, admits the utmost flexibility of diction, while at the same time insisting that each word shall carry, not *any* impression, but *the* impression that is sought. If the impression is one of splendor, then the splendid word is also the exact word. The protest is not, if I understand it, against this or that type or class of words *per se*, but against the use of any word solely for its adventitious values. That is in accord with the consistent usage of the great poets, and the Imagists are right in saying that their contention is not new. The renewed emphasis upon it is none the less wholesome, in spite of some obvious limitations and extremes in practice. We shall return to the matter, for the view under discussion is inextricably bound up with the whole question of *vers libre*. In the meantime, two or three passages from very recent poetry, Imagist and otherwise, may serve to bring out its catholicity with respect to diction. Here is a bit of Mr. Frost's "After Apple-Picking":

> My long two-pointed ladder's sticking through
>   a tree
> Toward heaven still,
> And there's a barrel that I did n't fill
> Beside it, and there may be two or three

Apples I did n't pick upon some bough.
But I am done with apple-picking now.
Essence of winter sleep is on the night,
The scent of apples: I am drowsing off.

Mr. Edwin Arlington Robinson thus writes
on cider barrels:

From one of them
A bright pine spile stuck out alluringly,
And on the black flat stone, just under it,
Glimmered a late-spilled proof that Archibald
Had spoken from unfeigned experience.
There was a fluted antique water-glass
Close by, and in it, prisoned, or at rest,
There was a cricket, of the brown soft sort
That feeds on darkness.

This is Miss Lowell:

I have whetted my brain until it is like a Damascus
      blade,
So keen that it nicks off the floating fringes of
      passers-by,
So sharp that the air would turn its edge
Were it to be twisted in flight.
Licking passions have bitten their arabesques
      into it,
And the mark of them lies, in and out,
Worm-like,
With the beauty of corroded copper patterning
      white steel.
My brain is curved like a scimitar,
And sighs at its cutting
Like a sickle mowing grass.

And here is another Imagist, Richard Aldington:

O Death,
Thou art an healing wind
That blowest over white flowers
A-tremble with dew;
Thou art a wind flowing
Over long leagues of lonely sea;
Thou art the dusk and the fragrance . . .
Thou art the silence of beauty,
And we look no more for the morning;
We yearn no more for the sun,
Since with thy white hands,
Death,
Thou crownest us with the pallid chaplets,
The slim colorless poppies
Which in thy garden alone
Softly thou gatherest.

And now still a third Imagist, Mr. John Gould Fletcher:

Whirlpools of purple and gold,
Winds from the mountains of cinnebar,
Lacquered mandarin moments, palanquins swaying
and balancing
Amid the vermilion pavilions, against the jade
balustrades.

In the evening I listen to the wind's lisping,
While the conflagrations of the sunset flicker and
clash behind me,
Flamboyant crenellations of glory amid the
charred ebony boles.

The new poetry, after all, is very like any other poetry, in the actual words that it uses — from "So keen that it nicks" to "flamboyant crenellations." Its insistence is upon the manner of their use. And that involves questions that will concern us later.

It is poetry, then, which, through its energizing influence, gives to words poetic quality; it is not poetic diction which makes poetry. If this were the truism that it seems to be, the critic's occupation would be gone.

VI

RHYME, METRE, AND VERS LIBRE

IT is true, I fear, that most of us who talk about the poet's craft are innocent of experience in its practice. "We never drank of Aganippe's well; Nor never did in shade of Tempe sit." Like Mephistopheles' philosopher in "Faust," who elucidates the mysteries of the weaver's craft, we're capable of a luminous demonstration of how the thing is done:

> The scholars praise it, but Lord love 'em,
> It has n't yet made weavers of 'em!

And so I often find myself leaning strongly towards a remark of Thomas Gray's to Mason: "You know I do not love, much less pique myself, on criticism, and think even a bad verse as good a thing or better than the best observation that ever was made upon it." Gray, to be sure, had begun his letter by saying that he was "almost blind with a great cold," and I'm inclined to think that his dictum must therefore be taken with a grain of allowance. But one may heartily agree that even the germs of creative energy are infinitely precious in a world where things are in the saddle and ride mankind, and one great verse alone outweighs a critic's volume. Yet criticism and creation do go hand in hand, and even the harmless, necessary expositor may sometimes have a place. And so, without a line of verse to bless myself withal, I still venture, most undogmatically, a few observations on the versifier's art.

Let me say at once, however, that I have no intention of going into the technicalities of verse. For one thing, that is something on which only the specialist has a right to speak, and I have no claim to expert knowledge in the intricate and baffling field of metrical technique. For another thing, the phase of the subject which concerns us here is independent of technical niceties. It is the bearing of certain broad and general considerations upon present problems that I wish to discuss. The view is vigorously urged to-day that rhyme and metre hamper the poet's free expression. It is that contention which I should like to examine, and the one object of this chapter is to attempt some answer to these questions: How far do rhyme and metre restrict the poet's freedom; and, as a corollary, wherein consists the peculiar freedom of free verse? That is really the central point at issue: the balance between restraint and liberty in art.

Let us recognize, without delay, that neither metre, in the strictest sense, nor rhyme, as we apply the term, is essential to poetry as such. Hebrew poetry, of course, had neither, and even the oldest English poetry was based on a rhythmic system other than that in use to-day. We are not concerned at the moment with their differences. For our immediate purpose, those are entirely immaterial. The essential point is that metrical forms are conventional, and therefore rest, like all matters of usage, on acceptance. They are open to change as any convention is open to change, and in the same way — namely, by a slow and gradual consent to something else. And the new thing will stand or fall according as it does or does not win its way into the permanent acceptance of the great community of readers, which moves together, if it move at all. The issue rests with the thing and the public. What you or I may say makes little difference.

Why say it, then? I confess that, like Wordsworth's little Edward, I am sometimes hard put to it for an answer. As I have already indicated, I am something of a fatalist when it comes to matters of convention. "But al shal passe that men prose or ryme; Take every man his turn, as for his tyme." Chaucer was wise, when he wrote

that, with the wisdom (and the humor) of experience. Eclipse and emergence in art go on incessantly, and always have. Nevertheless, underneath the inevitable flux there are permanencies.
And while conservatives hearten conservatives,
and radicals fire radicals to keener ardors, the
rest of us may at least endeavor to reach clearness.

As has been said, the point at issue is really that
of freedom. And we may first consider the extent
to which metre and rhyme impose restrictions
upon expression. That involves at once the relations between the rhythms of verse and those of
ordinary speech, when speech is touched with
emotion. For language wholly devoid of emotional quality does not enter into the question
at all.

The language of elevated thought or feeling is
always rhythmic. Strong feeling of whatever
sort, that is, imposes upon speech a rhythmic
beat. Even you and I, whose ordinary daily talk
maintains its slow or hurried, nervous or phleg-
matic, staccato or legato, but always pedestrian
gait — even you and I, under stress of compelling emotion, find our speech taking on not only
deeper color, but a more or less measured beat.
That rhythm is not the rhythm of verse; it is
infinitely more varied, less susceptible of formu-

lation, ebbing and flowing with the rise and fall of the emotion, controlled or unrestrained, that gives it being. And it is that heightening of rhythmic quality, whenever thought is deeply touched with feeling, that characterizes elevated prose.

In metrical verse, on the other hand, the rhythm follows relatively fixed patterns. In regular English metres the line is the salient unit, both to eye and ear, and the line is made up of a limited number of groups of stressed and unstressed syllables. Moreover, the number of unaccented syllables that may accompany an accented syllable is also limited. Beyond verse made up of varying alternations of one accented and one unaccented syllable, or of one accented and two unaccented syllables, English metre rarely goes. To state these obvious facts is to admit at once that metrical verse imposes restrictions upon the freedom of ordinary speech — which is merely to say in other words, that verse is a convention of art, whose very essence is restraint. It is contended, however, that this particular restraint is unduly rigid. Rhythmic utterance does not normally fall into units of fixed length, nor does it group its syllables inevitably by twos and threes. The protest is

not against *rhythm;* it is against imposing upon
rhythm the strait-jacket of *metre.* That is a perfectly intelligible position, and it is plausible to
the last degree. Its measure of justification is, I
think, neither so great as the radicals, nor so
slight as the conservatives, insist. At all events,
it is no merely academic question.

Now there is a fundamental fact which the
protestants, if I understand them, overlook.
Upon the length or the development of the larger,
infinitely varying rhythmic units, metre does not
impose any limitations whatever. These are free.
They are merely taken up into and merged with
another rhythmic movement. Let me make
clearer what I mean. The movement of regular
verse is a resultant, a resolution, of two rhythms,
one of which, taken alone, tends towards utter
freedom, the other of which, taken alone, tends
towards restraint. There is in verse, on the one
hand, the metrical unit — that is to say, for our
present purpose, the line. There is, on the other
hand, what we may designate as the sentence
rhythm or cadence. If the line length and the
sentence rhythm uniformly coincide (as they
do in some of Pope's couplets, for example) we
get monotony, deadly and intolerable. If there is
only the sentence cadence, without the beat of

the line, there is variety, but it is merely the variety of your speech and mine, when charged with emotion in varying degrees. Metrical verse, that is not sheer doggerel, is built upon the harmony of both. Behind the endlessly weaving rhythms of the sentence cadences beats steadily, in the best verse unobtrusively, the rhythm of the line. In the hands of the artist, the rhythmic cadences determined by the thought, or by the breath, or both, flow around and through and in the beat of the lines, but the beat of the lines is *there*, like time in music. The freedom of regular verse is the freedom of infinitely varied rhythms thrown against a constant rhythmic background. And the æsthetic pleasure of such verse lies largely in the conscious or unconscious recognition of unity in variety, of the fixed and constant taken up into the movement of the ever changing — in a word, in our inexhaustible human delight in the known and expected, when invested with the added charm of the unforeseen. The regular beat and the shifting rhythm — neither alone, but the two together — these constitute normal English verse. What free verse would strike out, to anticipate for a moment, is the recurrent rhythm of the line. Regular verse is the resultant of two rhythms, interwoven into innumerable harmonies. Free verse is built on one alone. That, broadly speaking, is the fundamental difference

I have said that the rhythm of the sentence or the phrase plays through and about the rhythm of the line, so that constantly shifting rhythmic patterns weave through the warp of the steadily beating metrical units. If you recall the second movement of Tschaikowsky's Pathetic Symphony, where the measured and muffled throbbing of the kettledrum holds its way without cessation through the surging rhythms of the orchestra, you will have one of a thousand musical analogues of the blending of the two rhythms in verse, which I am trying to make clear. Better still, let verse speak for itself. Here is a passage from Shakespeare, ruthlessly printed as if it were merely metrical lines. One rhythm, that is, has been torn bodily away from the other, in order that we may see with some clearness what is left:

> With fairest flowers.
> While summer lasts and I live here, Fidele.
> I'll sweeten thy sad grave. Thou shalt not lack.
> The flower that's like thy face, pale primrose, nor.
> The azur'd harebell, like thy veins, no, nor.
> The leaf of eglantine, whom not to slander.
> Out-sweeten'd not thy breath.

That, so read, is not verse, but a monstrosity.

Yet that is what must be, if metre really does impose itself as a restriction upon the larger freedom of rhythmic utterance. Of course it does not. Here is what Shakespeare wrote:

> With fairest flowers
> While summer lasts and I live here, Fidele,
> I'll sweeten thy sad grave. Thou shalt not lack
> The flower that's like thy face, pale primrose, nor
> The azur'd harebell, like thy veins, no, nor
> The leaf of eglantine, whom not to slander,
> Out-sweeten'd not thy breath.

The metrical units are there, but they are taken up into the larger rhythmic movement, to whose variety they impart a basic unity.

Or let us take two passages from one poet — a poet who is writing now, and who is catholic enough to practice in both kinds. One is a fully rhymed stanza in absolutely orthodox metre; the other is in *vers libre*. I shall not, at the moment, indicate which is which. Here is one.

> I followed her for long,
> With gazing eyes and stumbling feet.
> I cared not where she led me,
> My eyes were full of colors:
> Saffrons, rubies, the yellows of beryls,
> And the indigo-blue of quartz;
> Flights of rose, layers of chrysoprase,
> Points of orange, spirals of vermilion,
> The spotted gold of tiger-lily petals,
> The loud pink of bursting hydrangeas.

> I followed,
> And watched for the flashing of her wings.

And here is the other:

> The little apple leaves above their heads
> Let fall a quivering sunshine.
> Quiet, cool,
> In blossomed boughs they sat.
> Beyond, the beds of tulips blazed,
> A proper vestibule and antechamber to the
>   rainbow.
> Dyes of prismed richness:
> Carmine. Madder. Blues tinging dark browns
>   to purple.
> Silvers flushed to amethyst and tinct with gold.
> Round eyes of scarlet,
> Spotting tender saffron hues.
> Violets sunk to blacks,
> And reds in orange crushed.

The last (which I have arbitrarily printed as free verse) [1] is a regular, metrical, rhymed stanza. And its metrical pattern has imposed upon the rhythmic movement no more restriction, to the ear, than the unchartered freedom of the first. And it is for the ear, not for the eye, that poetry is written.

This is not a controversial document. It is an attempt, as unbiased as the academic mind per-

---

[1] The rhyme-words, which make it possible to restore the stanza, are: heads, cool, beds, vestibule, dyes, blues, flushed, eyes, hues, crushed.

mits, to state the facts. And one fact that has suffered temporary eclipse these days is the liberty inherent in the type of verse which is popularly supposed to cabin, crib, confine, bind in the poet's freedom of expression.

But metre imposes other checks on freedom. Words in normal speech, we are told, neither are so constructed in themselves, nor do they so fall into relation with each other, as to marshal the accented and unaccented syllables punctually at the proper intervals for the genesis of metrical feet. Yet the verse stress and the word stress must correspond. We may n't say "the fertile plains of Mésopótamía," though our rhythm cry out for it ever so loud. If we keep the rhythm, Mesopotamia must go overboard, and some such makeshift as "the fertile plains that bórder ón the Tígris" must take its place. And "border on the Tigris" may not be in the least what our scheme of things demands. Moreover, if we keep the words we want, we must often shift the order. If I 'm writing in a certain metre, I may n't say: "When Porphyria glided in, she straight shut out the cold and the storm." I must say:

> "When glided in Porphyria, straight
> She shut the cold out and the storm."

Granted at once both counts of the indictment!

Verse is *not* prose. But before I take the high ground that I propose to take on that point, let us look a little more closely at the facts.

In the first place, we do not *scan* English verse. The basis of English verse is accent, and accent, unlike classical quantity, is absolutely incapable of formulation. In the sentence I have just written, or in the one I am writing now, there are accented syllables of all degrees of stress, and there are likewise relatively unaccented syllables that carry more actual stress than some that are technically accented. There is one way, and only one, of correctly reading a Latin hexameter. There may be three or four ways of reading an English blank verse line. I venture to say that no two mortals ever read aloud any given long passage of verse with precisely the same rhythms. I am very sure that I should never read certain lines as the books on metrics say they should be read, and the metrists themselves read the same lines differently. And I seriously question if, for many lines, there is such a thing as a fixed reading. In other words, the state of things within the line is closely analogous to the situation we have seen in the case of the line and the circumambient sentence rhythm. There is for the line a general norm — iambic, trochaic, what you will — which carries through as a metrical background. But half the time we feel the norm merely as something which persists through shifting variations from it. And the idea of metre as a rigid locking up of rhythm into set and stereotyped forms, is the offspring of *a priori* notions, and not of the reading of great verse itself. The hampering influence of metre upon phrasal rhythm within the line has been rather grossly exaggerated these days, in the interest of a propaganda. Verse is not prose, let me say again; but neither is it a lock-step.

When we come to the dislocation of the normal order of words which is laid at the door of metrical necessity, we find a similar overstatement of the facts. Inversion undoubtedly occurs with unnecessary frequency in some English verse. "I have given up 'Hyperion,'" wrote Keats; "there were too many Miltonic inversions in it." "I hate inversions," declared Tennyson — a statement which, I fear, will lead some of the modernists forthwith to embrace them. The plain fact is that, relatively speaking, inversion in English verse is rare. Shifts in the position of words and phrases for the sake of emphasis are common — precisely as we practice them in prose. But the decided tendency of English verse, taken not here and there, but in the mass, is to preserve the normal word order. To illustrate adequately would be to print a dozen pages from a dozen poets, excluding one or two who do, by their individual usage, extend aid and comfort to the enemy. Here I may only instance a few random lines which, I think, it will none the less be admitted are typical. And I shall choose them from no one sort of poetry.

> Farewell! thou art too dear for my possessing,
> And like enough thou know'st thy estimate:
> The charter of thy worth gives thee releasing;
> My bonds in thee are all determinate.

> I long to talk with some old lover's ghost
> Who died before the god of love was born.

> But to our tale: Ae market night,
> Tam had got planted unco right;
> Fast by an ingle, bleezing finely,
> Wi' reaming swats, that drank divinely;
> And at his elbow, Souter Johnny,
> His ancient, trusty, drouthy crony;
> Tam lo'ed him like a vera brither;
> They had been fou for weeks thegither.

> Milton! thou should'st be living at this hour;
> England hath need of thee: she is a fen
> Of stagnant waters: altar, sword, and pen,
> Fireside, the heroic wealth of hall and bower,
> Have forfeited their ancient English dower
> Of inward happiness. We are selfish men.

Well! If the Bard was weather-wise, who made
  The grand old ballad of Sir Patrick Spence,
  This night, so tranquil now, will not go hence
Unroused by winds.

O what can ail thee, knight-at-arms,
  Alone and palely loitering?
The sedge is wither'd from the lake,
  And no birds sing.

       . . . for my purpose holds
To sail beyond the sunset, and the baths
Of all the western stars, until I die.
It may be that the gulfs will wash us down;
It may be we shall touch the Happy Isles,
And see the great Achilles, whom we knew.

Those are all as straightaway as your talk or mine, and they represent normal English verse. The contention that inversion is a necessity inherent in metre is a man of straw. That it is sometimes the path of least resistance is clear enough, and poets, like the rest of us, often take to their hurt the easy way. But that is rather the fault of the poet than of his medium.

But, insist the protestants, even though we grant all that, you are merely making the shoe pinch at another point. To keep the metre and avoid inversion still involves restriction, for we are not thereby relieved of the necessity of choosing words that fit the line. The limitation still persists. Undoubtedly it does. I have not the slightest intention of denying it. If I did, I should be denying that poetry was an art. And there is where I part company with some of my very good friends. Art demands a medium. That medium is never the same as the thing which it presents. Canvas is not a landscape, stone flesh, the stage reality. Obliterate the difference, and you have actuality, not art. We have already seen the grounds for this, and I shall not restate them here. Let the medium of poetry conform completely to the usages of ordinary speech, and it ceases to be poetry. If poetry is art, it must produce its effects through a medium which differentiates it, without divorcing it, from reality. It may not be unaccommodated speech. And that differentiation does without question impose restrictions upon the poet's absolute freedom of expression. But it is precisely these restrictions which make the poet.

> Wer Grosses will, muss sich zusammen raffen:
> *In der Beschränkung zeigt sich erst der Meister,*
> Und das Gesetz nur kann uns Freiheit geben.

Goethe has touched the core of the problem that confronts us now. The very restrictions of his medium become to the artist, as blank verse became growingly to Shakespeare, the way to

freedom; and the triumphs of art have been
through its sovereign dealings with the intractable, "when the hard means rebel." Let me continue my quotation:

> O Poet, then, forbear
>   The loosely-sandalled verse,
> Choose rather thou to wear
>   The buskin — strait and terse;
>
> Leave to the tiro's hand
>   The limp and shapeless style;
> See that thy form demand
>   The labor of the file. . . .
>
> Paint, chisel, then, or write;
>   But, that the work surpass,
> With the hard fashion fight, —
>   With the resisting mass.

Those are the words, not of a pedant or a peda-
gogue, but of Théophile Gautier. Let me set beside them — as artist's, not schoolmaster's witness again — a remark of Henry James from one
of those distilled prefaces of his. He is speaking
of the "charm of supreme difficulty" to the artist: "To put all that is possible of one's idea into
a form and compass that will contain and express
it only by delicate adjustments and an exquisite
chemistry, so that there will at the end be neither
a drop of one's liquor left nor a hair's breadth of

the rim of one's glass to spare — every artist will remember how often that sort of necessity has carried with it its particular inspiration." That is written of fiction, but it is supremely true of verse. And verse foregoes its limitations at its peril. For art gambles with that which makes it art, when it rebels against restriction.

But we are not yet done with the shackles. There is still rhyme. And we shall consider that as we have considered metre, only in its relation to freedom of expression.

In the first place, rhyme is, of course, an accident rather than an essential of verse. And it is scarcely necessary to point out that the term rhyme, in its popular acceptance, refers to what is technically known as end rhyme. Strictly speaking, alliteration is rhyme too — that is to say, it is initial, as contrasted with end rhyme. But the technical distinction need not concern us here. By rhyme I mean what we all mean in ordinary usage — similarity or identity, as between two words or even sets of words, of an accented vowel sound and whatever follows it, set off by difference in the preceding sound. And rhyme, thus understood, does several things.

For one thing, it gives the sort of æsthetic pleasure which arises from the recognition of sameness with difference — the pleasure which, in another fashion, metre itself affords. Let me illustrate what I mean from an unrhymed poem. The first line of Collins's "Ode to Evening" is this:

If aught of oaten stop, or pastoral song.

If, now, you do what I am certain Collins never did — namely, write out the consonant sounds of the line, you find a remarkable result. Here it is: f t f t (n) st p r p st r (l s ng). The same consonants are repeated in a sequence which resembles a mathematical design. But observe: the recurrences of identical consonants are accompanied by totally different vowel sounds — by a vowel sequence, in fact, as remarkable as the consonantal sequence, ranging from the full open sound of "aught," down through "oat" and "stop," to the lighter *o* in "pastoral," and up again in "song." The music of the line, in other words —

If aught of oaten stop, or pastoral song —

is due to the nice conjunction of recurring consonants with subtly varying vowels. And if one cares to see the difference between such an effect and that of crass identity, one has only to read the next line as Collins first wrote it:

May hope, O pensive Eve, to sooth thine ear.

There "hope O pe" is sheer cacophony, and "sive Eve" little better. And Collins, whose ear was exquisite to a degree, changed the line to read:

May hope, chaste Eve, to sooth thy modest ear —

sacrificing "pensive" on the altar of musical effect.

Now rhyme, by a similar merging of sameness with difference, gives a specific sort of æsthetic pleasure, and that, I take it, is its *raison d'être*. It does, however, other more or less useful things. It obviously sets off the metrical unit, the line; and, paradoxically enough, it also binds lines together in larger units — couplets, quatrains, or what not. For the first sound still echoes in the ear when its counterpart occurs, and the two link together, in varying degrees according to the interval, their respective lines. Rhyme plays, then, a rather important, though not an essential part in verse.

But rhyme, in the nature of the case, imposes restrictions upon the poet's liberty. The number of words in the language that rhyme with any given word is obviously limited. The use of a word in rhyme, accordingly, compels the poet to choose a second word, not for its sense alone, but for its sound. And even so, his range of choice is circumscribed by a purely accidental fact — the number of rhyming words which actually exist. Only a fanatic would deny that this constitutes a definite restraint upon free choice, and nobody that I know of does deny it. The poets themselves have grumbled freely. Chaucer translates three Balades of Oton de Granson, and ends his envoy thus:

> And eek to me it is a greet penaunce,
> Sith rym in English hath swich scarsitee,
> To folwe word by word the curiositee
> Of Graunson, floure of hem that make in Fraunce.

I pass over reluctantly the battles royal that the sixteenth and seventeenth centuries waged on the subject, with Spenser and Gabriel Harvey, Campion and Daniel, among the protagonists. Dryden speaks of "the slavery of rhyme," and of "the close of that one syllable, which often confines, and more often corrupts, the sense of all the rest." Gray characterizes lyric style in words which I wonder that the Imagists have not appropriated as their motto: "Extreme conciseness of expression, yet pure, perspicuous, and musical." "This," he goes on, "I have always aimed at, and never could attain; the necessity of rhyming is one great obstacle to it." *Per contra,*

Robert Lloyd protests, in some rhymes "On Rhyme," that

> While the trim bard in easy strains,
> Talks much of fetters, clogs, and chains;
> He only aims that you should think,
> How charmingly he makes them clink.

But of sterner stuff is Quevedo's "Complaint of the Poets in Hell":

> Oh, this damn'd Trade of Versifying,
> Has brought us all to Hell for lying!
> For writing what we do not think,
> Merely to hear the Verse cry Clink;
> For rather than abuse the Meter,
> Black shall be white, Paul shall be Peter.

And I would there were space to quote from the Reverend John Edwards, the Paul, the Augustine, the Bradwardine, the Calvin of his day, as his admirers called him, the passage which begins: "Verse is Words put into a Wanton-Posture," and ends: "Those who are excessively addicted to [Rhyme] have generally their Minds and Manners distorted. This Poetic Age hath prov'd the most Atheistical and Immoral." "Truly," one might say to rhyme, as Touchstone to Corin, "truly, thou art damm'd. . . . thou art in a parlous state."

And it would be easy to accumulate corroborative evidence from the poets themselves —

especially if, to make a case, we levy on their Juvenilia:

> Memory! dear enchanter!
>   Why bring back to view
> Dreams of youth, which banter
>   All that e'er was true?

That is Tennyson at the age of sixteen or so, and "banter" dances to "enchanter's" piping, since "canter" was the sole alternative left open to the dreams of youth. Keats's trees sprout "a shady *boon* For simple sheep" under the obvious compulsion of the *moon;* and his solitary thinkings "*dodge* Conception to the very bourne of heaven," because they can't dodge "*lodge*" in the preceding line. The Alps in "Childe Harold" are endowed with scalps, since even Walker's Lexicon could give no help. Marjorie Fleming's divine candor is shared by few of her fellow-craftsmen:

> He was kill'd by a cannon splinter
> Quite in the middle of the winter,
> (Perhaps it was not at that time,
> But I can get no other rhyme).

Of course the difficulty puts adventurous spirits on their mettle. Browning said he thought he could make a rhyme for every word in the English language, and you may read in the Tennyson "Memoir" his *tours de force* on rhinoceros,

Ecclefechan, and Craigenputtock. And everybody knows Byron's

> But — Oh! ye lords of ladies intellectual,
> Inform us truly, have they not hen-peck'd you all?

But that is amiable license and not liberty.

I have now played the devil's advocate with
exemplary thoroughness. Rhyme restricts the
poet's freedom. Very good; so be it. The sole
question is, how far the game is worth the candle.
Admitting losses, are there countervailing gains?
For the law of compensation rules supreme in
art, as it holds sway in life, and you cannot eat
your cake in poetry, and have it too. Abandon
rhyme, and the lady (I am quoting Hamlet!)
shall say her mind more freely. Will she, or he,
however, say it with more beauty? Will it even
necessarily be said more exactly? Sometimes,
yes! But one of the curious phenomena of language is the uncanny way in which sound and
sense have the trick of playing into each other's
hands. The disclosure of a sort of Leibnitzian
preëstablished harmony between rhyme and reason is one of the prerogatives of the poetic gift.
And some of the most felicitous turns of thought
and phrase in poetry are the result of a flash of
inspiration under the happy guidance of a rhyme.

That is not an offhand statement, but I must confine myself for illustration to a single case in point. In the sonnet "On first looking into Chapman's Homer," Keats first wrote:

> Oft of one wide expanse had I been told
>> That deep-brow'd Homer ruled as his demesne;
>> *Yet could I never judge what men could mean,*
> Till I heard Chapman speak out loud and bold

Then the nine low words that crept in one dull line: "Yet could I never judge what men could mean" — gave place, under the compulsion of the rhyme, to the splendid phrase which now completes the figure:

> Oft of one wide expanse had I been told
>> That deep-brow'd Homer ruled as his demesne;
>> *Yet did I never breathe its pure serene,*
> Till I heard Chapman speak out loud and bold.

That is one instance out of hundreds, of the happiness in words which rhyming often hits on, which reason itself could not so prosperously be delivered of.

In a word, poetry, regarded from the side of its technique, is the moulding of language to artistic ends. It deals with the æsthetic as well as the significative values of words. In so far as the two sets of values do not clash, rhyme enhances that power of awakening delight which verse shares with music. If the values conflict, rhyme has no case. But it is part of the poet's challenging and obdurate enterprise to see that they do not conflict. Rhyme simply affords him what Byron sought in the study of Armenian: it offers him something craggy for his mind to break on. And whether they take the form of rhyme or metre, or of something else, I confess to a firm belief in the tonic properties of crags.

Moreover, the other function of rhyme is something which poetry can ill afford to spare. For rhyme is one of the binding elements in both the production and the perception of structural unity. Great poetry is vertebrate. Cogency and consecutiveness of development are as characteristic of the supreme lyrics, even, as are rhythm and imagery. Creative energy in its highest exercise is magnificently architectonic, and it imposes upon the lyric impulse an ordered sequence and an organic unity. For the great poets have not only thought straight themselves, even when they felt most deeply, but they have also made it incumbent on us to think straight after them. And rhyme is a powerful factor in throwing into relief what Pope would call "the strong connections, nice dependencies, gradations just," which constitute a poem an artistic whole. I am well aware that there are those who will reject my major premise. If one prefer (as one may) Debussy to Beethoven, or Gauguin to Rembrandt, one may, quite intelligibly, care little for firm structural line in poetry. If we recognize at all, however, that beauty of form which consists in a sequence of balanced parts composing into an ordered unity, we shall also recognize the constructive value of rhyme. It would be difficult to imagine the superb cogency of the "Divine Comedy" apart from the welding power of the *terza rima*. And to pass to one of the briefest and at the same time most flawless of all lyrics, I shall ask you to observe not merely the music, but also the synthesizing effect of the rhymes in Goethe's lines:

> Ueber allen Gipfeln
> Ist Ruh;
> In allen Wipfeln
> Spürest du
> Kaum einen Hauch;
> Die Vögelein schweigen im Walde.
> Warte nur, balde
> Ruhest du auch.

Rob that of its rhymes, and you obliterate its very essence. Or consider the first stanza at which my "Oxford Book of English Verse" happens to open:

Have you seen but a bright lily grow
  Before rude hands have touch'd it?
Have you mark'd but the fall of the snow
  Before the soil hath smutch'd it?
Have you felt the wool of beaver,
    Or swan's down ever?
Or have smelt o' the bud o' the brier,
    Or the nard in the fire?
Or have tasted the bag of the bee?
O so white, O so soft, O so sweet is she!

That, too, is slight, if you will; but its structure is as firm as it is delicate, and the design is pricked out, so to speak, by the rhymes.

I need scarcely add, I hope, that a poem may possess artistic unity of high order, without the aid of rhyme. But it is no less true that rhyme has become in English poetry a constructive element of great value, and may not be discarded without loss. Whether there are compensatory gains is another question, which we shall come to in a moment.

The conventional forms of English verse, accordingly, do not shackle poetry so disastrously as we are sometimes asked to believe. On the contrary, the very limitations frequently become in a true sense creative agencies. But it does not follow that the door is therefore closed to fresh adventures in technique. And such an adventure is now in full career.

It is, among other things, a frank revolt against metrical conventions, and, like all insurgent tendencies, it is extreme. But it is also constructive, and it is experimenting in a genuinely fruitful fashion. At its best, it is a serious attempt to readjust the relations of content and form in poetry, and as such it is worthy of the most respectful consideration. At its worst, it is no more absurd than scores of its predecessors, long since embalmed among the curiosities of literature. The movement is neither a bogy nor an avatar. It is merely part and parcel of the intellectual ferment of our day — one more wave in the endless ebb and flow of action and reaction, the infinitesimal increments of which we call Progress. And criticism has no cause to scoff, even though it may not feel called upon to pray. To understand, so far as possible, and to appraise are more to the point.

But both understanding and appraisal are extremely difficult. For one thing, we are too close for perspective. I have tried to establish a general background, but even at that we are still in too close proximity to the picture. Contemporary judgments, pro or con, are notorious even among time's laughing-stocks. And one of the most quintessential of time's little ironies is its trick of extinguishing *us*, through the very process of providing us with due perspective. Yet we can't wait till we're dead, to make up our transitory minds. We must speak now, or forever after hold our peace.

Moreover, clarity and poise of judgment in this particular instance are rendered almost unattainable through the fact that the movement we are concerned with is beset with innumerable cross currents and shifting channels. The new poets themselves are far from unanimous in either theory or practice. There are wings extreme to the point of anarchy — the Paroxysmists in France, the Vorticists in England, and mild lunacies of one sort or another in this country. There is also, within the insurgent camp itself, an unobtrusive but unmistakable reaction from these extremes, out of which has emerged a relatively moderate and balanced Centre. And there are gradations all the way between. And since one group repudiates what another group stands sponsor for, it is sometimes difficult in a brief discussion to avoid, without interminable qualifications and abatements, a certain appearance of unfairness. That, I fear, is inevitable.

As for myself, taking the insurgents by and large, I have profound respect for certain of their aims, and I admire tremendously some things that they have done. But I doubt the validity of some of their assertions, and I do not wholly share their implicit faith in their own methods, or their pardonable family pride in all their off-spring. I shall briefly indicate what seem to me both gains and losses.

It is their metrical tenets that concern us now. And it is not my purpose to discuss either the origins or the history of *vers libre*. It is sufficient to say that the present impulse comes primarily from France; that it found, when it came, the ground prepared for it in differing ways by Arnold, and Whitman, and Henley, and others; and that it has since passed, or is passing, both directly and at second-hand, under the influence of Greek, Chinese and Japanese, and even Hebrew poetry. Its history, in a word, is absolutely typical of the procedure of English poetry from the Middle Ages on, in that it represents the grafting of foreign scions upon the native stock. So far as its behavior in this respect is concerned, it is maintaining the established traditions of English poetry.

When one asks precisely what free verse *is*, the answer is more difficult. Miss Amy Lowell has been at more pains than anybody else to define and to explain it; and in the Preface to "Sword Blades and Poppy Seed"; in the *North American Review* for January, 1917; in the closing chapter of her recent volume, "Tendencies in Modern American Poetry"; and still more recently in the *Dial* (January 17, 1918), she has made it as clear as it probably can be made. And I shall draw for my statement upon these documents.

"The definition of *vers libre* is: a verse-form based upon cadence." But cadence is not metre. "To understand *vers libre*, one must abandon all desire to find in it the even rhythm of metrical feet. One must allow the lines to flow as they will when read aloud by an intelligent reader." Or, to put it another way, unrhymed cadence is "built upon 'organic rhythm,' or the rhythm of the speaking voice with its necessity for breathing, rather than upon a strict metrical system." "Free verse *within its own law of cadence* has no absolute rules; it would not be 'free' if it had." What is this law of cadence? For that is the vital point. I shall still essay no statement of my own. "The unit of *vers libre* is not the foot, the number of the syllables, the quantity, or the line. The unit is the strophe, which may be the whole poem, or may be only a part. Each strophe is a complete circle." The emphasis, then (and this is fundamental), is upon what has been elsewhere called "the desire of verse to *return upon itself*." The law of cadence, accordingly, if I understand it, applies to a balanced flow of free rhythm, of which any given *line* is but a part. *The group of lines* constitutes the unit, which is a rhythmic movement returning upon itself, like the swing of a balanced pendulum. Within that swing, the lines move as the poet wills. The poem "can be fast or slow, it may even jerk, but this perfect swing it must have; even its jerks must follow the central movement." This summary is, I believe, a perfectly fair statement of the insurgent position. It is not my own, except in the selection and arrangement of the excerpts, and in that I have been scrupulously careful to wrest nothing from its context.

Now this represents free verse as its serious practitioners understand it. And it is with this alone that I am concerned. The chopped-up prose that goes by the same name is worth neither your time nor mine for critical consideration. The genuine attempt to work out a new artistic medium has suffered from the confusion, and I am glad to emphasize the difference. I have read most of the best and, led on by an unholy fascination, far more than my quota of the worst

free verse printed in recent years, and I speak by
the book. And now for the more serious experiment itself.

Free verse, as just defined, is at its best essentially *strophic*. It is a larger rhythmic movement
which subsumes other rhythms. Regular verse
is also at its best essentially strophic. It too, as
I have already tried to make clear, is a larger
rhythmic movement which subsumes other
rhythms. The two have in common, then, an
enveloping rhythm. What is the difference?
Mainly this: in the one, the constituent rhythmic elements, namely metrical lines, have a relatively uniform beat; in the other, they are free to
vary as they please. Therein lies the peculiar
freedom of free verse. It is not in the strophic
element as such. That it has in common with
regular verse. The great strophic rhythms of
"Paradise Lost," for example, which are far
more significant than the rhythms of Milton's
lines, are as free as the strophic rhythms of any
poem in *vers libre*. The sentence and phrasal
rhythms of the great rhymed lyrics are always
potentially, and in many cases actually, as unrestrained as the modern cadences. What the
modern unrhymed cadences abandon, as I have
already said, is the recurrent beat of the line. It

is here that they have freed themselves from a
partially real and partially supposed restraint.
The constituent elements of the strophic rhythm
need not, as in regular verse, be uniform.

Where lies the gain? The answer to that involves the other tenets of the movement. For
free verse (and I am still speaking only of the
more artistic use of it) may not fairly be separated
from its content. The poets who use it insist that
they see the world in their own way, and they
have hit upon a medium which they believe
serves best to record their impressions of what
they see. And they have a right to ask, as they
do, that this fact be taken into account. How,
then, does the New Poetry envisage its world?

For one thing, it sets itself in sharp opposition
to what it calls "the cosmic poet," who indulges
in vague generalities, magnificent and sonorous,
about his universe. The new, especially the
Imagist poetry "concerns itself with man in his
proper relation to the universe, rather than as the
lord and master of it." The insurgent poets, as
one of them has put it, are children of a scientific
age. They know that man is not the centre of the
universe, and so they scrupulously refrain from
any attempt to impose their feelings upon things.
And one of their chief aims, accordingly, is the

attainment of what they have variously called externality, exteriority, objectivity, or immediacy. That means, in turn, that their chief end in expression is clearness and hardness of presentation, "discarding . . . all extraneous detail which tends to blur . . . the vividness of the main theme." And finally, their search is for "the exact word," the word that at once presents the thing and conveys the writer's impression of it to the reader. That is a consistent and reasoned doctrine of the poet's business, and it cannot be dismissed with a gesture.

Unrhymed cadence, then, is felt to serve these ends with peculiar aptness. It imposes no restriction upon the choice of words, since within the strophic movement the rhythm is variable at will, and no accentual idiosyncrasies need bar a refractory but inevitable word from its meet place. By the same token, the temptation to employ inversions ceases to operate. And finally, the rhythms, bare as they are of conventional emotional associations, are a *tabula rasa* on which the poet may inscribe his own sharp and clear impressions for conveyance, in their pristine freshness, to the reader.

Before coming to debit and credit, I must avow a certain skepticism on one important point.

I do not believe that *vers libre* has nearly the advantage over metre that is claimed for it in the choice of the *mot juste*. If it is merely a matter of relative *ease* that is involved, I yield the point at once. But ease in art is not a high desideratum; we are concerned with the results. And over against every example of the inevitable word in unrhymed cadence (and the number is happily large), may be set "exact" words, not single spies but in battalions, from metrical verse. Given a rich vocabulary and the artist's sense for words, and metre will interpose little or no obstacle to the *mot juste*. The diction of Mr. Robinson and Mr. Frost — to leave William Shakespeare and a few others out of account — is quite as exact, in the full Imagist sense of the term, as the diction of H. D. or Richard Aldington, and the blank verse does n't halt for it either. I am talking of artists, of course. Neither free verse will save, nor metre damn, the others.

As for profit and loss, I have no hesitation in saying that in my judgment the serious practitioners of *vers libre* are making contributions of genuine significance to English poetry. I also believe that over against this indebtedness must be set certain definite abatements. Let us take the contributions first.

It is the freshness and vividness of the diction, in the best free verse, that is of particular worth just now to poetry. Less, indeed, than is constantly insisted, but still to an unfortunate degree, poetry *has* been tending to become vague, and nebulous, and stereotyped in its vocabulary. And it is a relief to come to a diction that is frequently crisp, and incisive, and terse, and (if you will) *external*. The vocabulary of poetry is undergoing a renovation. And only the captious can well decline to admit the fact, or to recognize the significance of what is happening.

Furthermore, wherever the new rhythms are to be classified — and that is a question which will concern us later — they constitute, in competent hands, a medium of unmistakable artistic possibilities. And they are sometimes very beautiful. There are even stern traditionalists who cherish a surreptitious liking for the thing, enhanced by the pleasantly uneasy sense that it ought n't to be liked. When that happens, tradition must rub the sleep out of its eyes, and accept the challenge that bids nor sit nor stand, but go. And that in itself is reason enough for those of us who love the old to bid a hearty welcome to the new.

But that welcome does not absolve us from a

critical scrutiny of the other side of the account. And there are two points in particular which give one pause. In the first place, the trend of recent poetry towards what it calls externality, results in the virtual exclusion of much that is no less the stuff of creative art. I sympathize profoundly with a poetry that does n't make a pageant of its bleeding heart, or that even declines to wear its heart, bleeding or not, on its sleeve. But children of a scientific and analytic age though we may be, and however fruitful our exploiting of the field of the external and the concrete, it still remains true that we are children of more ages than our own. Intellectually, the contention of the New Poetry has some validity; with respect to that which lies deeper than the intellectual — I distrust the word, or I should say with respect to the spiritual — the case is not so clear. There are still "exultations, agonies, And love, and man's unconquerable mind," and no recoil from the so-called "cosmic" releases poetry from its wrestlings with these, except to its grave loss. I know that the poets insist that they are not excluded; that the concrete and the external are merely, in their work, the medium through which the informing spirit is expressed. In a measure that is true. But the medium itself is so alluring, and the delight in pure sensation so acute, that the suggestions and impressions which do reach us stir certain regions of consciousness alone, and leave the depths unmoved. I am not quarrelling with the squirrel because it is not a mountain, nor judging Imagism by a standard that is not its own. I am merely insisting that there are also other standards, valid still, and that the old fields have not yet been exhausted. I yield to no one in my admiration for the chiselled, pellucid beauty of many an image that lends distinction to the best work of the new school. But the peril to the movement at the hands of its most notable exponents lies, as I see it, in an over-preoccupation with an exquisite craftsmanship in verbal textures — a craftsmanship which in its own way sometimes rivals that of the Flemish painters. Of such technique there can scarcely be too much in a slipshod world; but the self-imposed restriction of that technique to the expression of sheer immediacy of experience is a grave limitation. This at least is the dispassionate judgment of a not unsympathetic reader.

As for the rhythms of free verse, my genuine liking for many of them is also tempered by a doubt. One feels in the new verse — and one is meant to feel it — the absence of a norm. Yet freedom is felt as the freedom of *art*, only when it is exercised within restraint. The restraining rhythms of the free verse strophe, to be sure, are there, but they are themselves unrestrained, except by an inner compulsion of their own. And that compulsion is felt at all, it would seem, only by the finer craftsmen of the *genre*. In the mass of what answers to the name of free verse, the "quality of return" is absent. In so far, then, as the experiment keeps clearly before it the ineluctable necessity of a moulding *form*, even though that form have not as yet received the sanction of tradition, its warrant is secure. Its peril in this direction lies in a tendency to obliterate the ancient landmarks between freedom and license. And even at its best, in electing this peculiar freedom of its own, *vers libre* has at the same time made certain definite renunciations. For by substituting rhythm alone for the fusion of rhythm and metre in one, it has foregone the great harmonic, orchestral effects of the older verse. That it has a perfect right to do; but the compensations which it has to offer must be clear.

I do not wish to close without saying what in my judgment is the thing that after all most demands expression. Far more significant than the faults of the movement, or even than its merits, is the fact that it *exists*. At no time, perhaps, in the history of this country at least, has there been so keen and widespread an interest in poetry. We may carp at the form that it takes, we may poke fun at its vagaries, we may leave it, if we please, unread. The fact remains that more people are reading poetry to-day than for a period of many years. That in itself is of happy omen. You can't steer a boat that is n't moving. Once let it gather headway, and the rudder will do its part. The new preoccupation with poetry in this country is a fact of large significance — not so much for what the poetry itself now is, as for what it promises. Many of us have been free with criticism and suggestion, not because we do not believe in the importance of the movement, but because we do. The critic, usually, does not produce — as he is often told in no uncertain terms. The poet, on the other hand, is apt to lack the detachment which alone makes fruitful criticism possible. The two must work together to a common end. If they do — if the new poets can bring themselves to moderate their attitude of somewhat sensitive resentment towards those who call their art in question; if the critics, on their part, can forego their not infrequent tone of irritating condescension, and welcome, with no surrender of discrimination, a fresh impulse — if this fraternity of interests can be brought from Utopia to Earth, we may look with some assurance for a genuine poetic Renaissance.

VII

THE great uncharted region in the realm of letters is the borderland between poetry and prose. It has been for centuries the Debatable Ground, the No Man's Land of literature, claimed now by one side, now by the other, and securely held by neither. Is all speech that possesses imaginative quality poetry, or must it have rhythm too? If "Paradise Lost" is poetry, why not the great purple patches of the "Areopagitica"? If Chaucer's "Troilus and Creseyde," why not "Tom Jones"? "There have been many most excellent poets that never versified," declared Sir Philip Sidney, adding, however, a *quid pro quo:* "and now swarm many versifiers that need never answer to the name of poets." "Plato was essentially a poet," says Shelley; "Lord Bacon was a poet." The pretty battle of the books has raged since Aristotle, with all the fine fury that attends a bloodless combat. And the Homeric bead-roll of the protagonists, and their acts, and how they warred, behold they are written in the second chapter of Professor Gummere's notable volume on the "Beginnings of Poetry." There you may read, in racy summary, the arguments pro and con. I have no desire, and there is no occasion, to ride into the lists. All that need be said here is this: We use the word "poetry," as we use hundreds of other words, in a loose as well as in a more rigid sense. When we accord ourselves an entirely permissible latitude, we may say with Keats that "the poetry of earth is never dead"; we may assert with Blackie that "to live poetry is always better than to write it"; we may affirm with perfect propriety and truth that all language is poetry. But as a matter of usage merely, if we speak of poetry without qualification or saving clause, we are commonly understood to have reference to both an imaginative and a rhythmic use of speech. We do not, as a rule, include prose.

But we may not wisely whistle before we are out of the woods. For prose may be rhythmic too. And that brings us to the really fundamental distinction — a distinction which, unlike the other, has more than academic interest. The important contradistinction is not that of poetry and prose, but the antithesis of prose and *verse*. That eliminates the common factors, and reduces

the problem to one of form. And until recently
our feet were on firm ground. "The only strict
antithesis to Prose is Metre," wrote Wordsworth.
That is neat and satisfactory to the last degree.
Prose may be and verse is rhythmic; but verse
is always and prose never metrical. Metre becomes, accordingly, the exact and scientific differentia between verse and prose. But now a respectable body of verse turns its back on metre
and walks out. Does it remain verse? If it does,
what is now its differentia? Rhythm is not, for
prose may be rhythmic. Metre is not, for it has
thrown metre to the dogs. How does the rhythm
of emancipated verse differ from the rhythm of
elevated prose? That is the disconcerting question which confronts us, and it is a question from
which there is no escape.

Now elevated prose may be strongly rhythmic,
but we still think of it as prose, never as verse.

Intreat me not to leave thee, or to return from following after thee: for whither thou goest, I will go; and
where thou lodgest, I will lodge: thy people shall be my
people, and thy God my God: where thou diest, will I
die, and there will I be buried: the Lord do so to me,
and more also, if ought but death part thee and me.

Underneath that runs the balanced structure of
the Hebrew poetry which it is, but it is a trans-

lation into the noble rhythms of surpassingly perfect prose. It is not verse.

> O eloquent, just, and mighty Death! whom none could advise, thou hast persuaded; what none hath dared, thou hast done; and whom all the world hath flattered, thou only hast cast out of the world and despised: thou hast drawn together all the far-stretched greatness, all the pride, cruelty, and ambition of man, and covered it all over with these two narrow words, *Hic jacet.*

Raleigh's apostrophe is majestic in its rhythm beyond all but the greatest verse, but its cadences are still the cadences of prose. No one could possibly mistake it for anything else. Or take the haunting close of Sir Thomas Browne's "Garden of Cyrus":

> Nor will the sweetest delight of Gardens afford much comfort in Sleep, wherein the dullness of that Sense shakes hands with delectable Odours; and though in the bed of *Cleopatra*, can hardly with any delight raise up the ghost of a Rose. . . . But who can be drowsie at that hour which freed us from everlasting sleep? or have slumbring thoughts at that time when Sleep itself must end, and, as some conjecture, all shall awake again?

We may call that poetry, if we please; we should never think of describing it as verse.

But these represent the uncertain glories of the Elizabethan and Jacobean prose — the surging cadences which, after the reaction of the eighteenth century, appeared again with other contours in De Quincey and Carlyle and Ruskin, and now have vanished. The rhythms of modern artistic prose are simpler. Now they are like this of Pater's: [1]

> The perfume
> Of the little flowers of the lime-tree
> Fell through the air upon them,
> Like rain;
> While time seemed to move ever more slowly
> To the murmur of the bees in it,
> Till it almost stood still
> On June afternoons.

Now the rhythms are like these of Joseph Conrad:

> The bright domes
> Of the parasols
> Swayed lightly outwards
> Like full-blown blossoms
> On the rim of a vase . . .

> The wheels turned solemnly;
> One after another the sunshades drooped,
> Folding their colors
> Like gorgeous flowers shutting their petals
> At the end of the day.

Again there are cadences of almost languorous beauty as in these of Fiona Macleod:

[1] I have intentionally printed the prose that follows in such fashion as to bring out its cadences to the eye.

The gloaming came,
Silverly.
The dew glistened
On the fronds of the ferns,
In the cups of the moss.
The stars
Emerged delicately,
As the eyes of fawns
Shining through the green gloom
Of the forest . . .
A cool green freshness
Came into the air.
The stars
Were as wind-whirled fruit
Blown upward from the tree-tops.
The moon,
Full-orbed and with a pulse of flame,
Led a tide of soft light
Across the brown shores of the world . . .
A doe,
Heavy with fawn,
Lay down among the dewy fern,
And was at peace.

Here, with a stronger rhythm, is Maurice Hewlett:

As he had seen her,
So he painted . . .
A grey, translucent sea
Laps silently
Upon a little creek
And, in the hush of a still dawn,
The myrtles and sedges on the water's brim
Are quiet . . .

> She would vanish, we know,
> Into the daffodils
> Or a bank of violets.
> And you might tell her presence there,
> Or in the rustle of the myrtles,
> Or coo of doves
> Mating in the pines;
> You might feel her genius
> In the scent of the earth
> Or the kiss of the West wind;
> But you could only see her
> In mid-April,
> And you should look for her
> Over the sea.

What is it really that we have been reading? If I had not given due notice, I think you would promptly say, Free verse. There has been no juggling of the cards. We have merely been paying strict attention to the "'organic rhythm,' or the rhythm of the speaking voice," and allowing the phrases (still to quote a well-known description of free verse) "to flow as they will when read aloud by an intelligent reader." Let me complete the quotation: "Then new rhythms will become evident — satisfying, and delightful. For this poetry definitely harks back to the old oral tradition; it is written to be spoken. For we believe that poetry is a spoken, not a written art." That is sound doctrine. But do not these satisfying and delightful rhythms (as they are) appear in what we have just read? And that still, rightly or wrongly, goes by the name of prose.

I am not, let me say most emphatically, bringing an indictment against *vers libre*, or seeking to filch from it its name. I am trying, as a somewhat mystified admirer, to detect its specific differences. Metre is gone. Its cadences are either the cadences of rhythmic prose, or they are not. If they are not, some difference should be obvious to the ear. What we have so far read does not form a fair test, because for it the only standard of comparison is our vague recollection of the general effect of free verse rhythms. Let us put free verse and modern rhythmic prose in immediate juxtaposition. The ear is the sole judge. Beyond the law of the strophic rhythm, we are told, free verse has no absolute rules, since it would not be "free" if it did. We are therefore compelled to become empiricists.

Three years ago, I printed in the *Nation* a brief article called "An Unacknowledged Imagist." In it I quoted a remark of Mr. Witter Bynner's: "George Meredith has thousands of Imagist poems incidental to each of his novels." Having observed this myself, not perhaps by thousands, but at least by scores, it occurred to

me to put the statement to a test. Their lucid
clarity (if I may repeat a few sentences of what
I then said), their texture "dur et rare," their
marvellous fidelity to the particular fact, above
all, their depth of imaginative insight — all this
was obvious enough. There were images that
suggested the clairvoyance of a crystal gazer;
images with the luminous precision of a bit of
landscape seen in the reflex of a lens; images that
"quintessentialized an emotion until it burnt
white hot," images crisp, incised, penetrating,
"strait and terse." But did they fulfil the other
requirements of Imagist verse? Did they have
"the quality of *return* . . . the balance which
produces the effect of music upon the ear"? In
other words did they have the *strophic* character
which constitutes the law of cadence of free
verse?

Let us set side by side, then, a few passages of
Meredith's prose and a few bits of Imagist verse,
and compare the cadences. In none of the Mere-
dithean excerpts have I varied from the original
by a syllable, and I have chosen the *vers libre* for
its beauty. I have no desire to make a case by
setting good prose over against bad verse.

> Her face was like the after-sunset
> Across a rose-garden,

With the wings of an eagle
Poised outspread on the light.

The light of her face falls from its flower,
as a hyacinth,
hidden in a far valley,
perishes upon burnt grass.

The two fragments are alike beautiful; they are alike strophic. But the first is from Meredith's "Sandra Belloni," the second from a poem in *vers libre* by H. D. Let us dwell for a moment on two more faces:

He had a look
Superior to simple strength and grace:
The look
Of a great sky-bird
About to mount.

In your eyes
Smoulder the fallen roses of out-lived minutes,
And the perfume of your soul
Is vague and suffusing,
With the pungence of sealed spice-jars.

Both things of beauty in image and rhythm. George Meredith's is written as prose; Miss Lowell's as verse.

She had the secret
Of lake waters under rock,
Unfathomable
In limpidness.

> She has new leaves
> After her dead flowers,
> Like the little almond tree
> Which the frost hurt.

The first, precisely as it stands, is from Meredith's prose; the second is a complete poem in *vers libre* by Richard Aldington; and the strophic rhythm in each is obvious to any ear. Listen once more to the "return . . . the balance which produces the effect of music on the ear":

> He was like a Tartar
> Modelled by a Greek:
> Supple
> As the Scythian's bow,
> Braced
> As the string!

That is Meredith. And here is H. D. again:

> Sand cuts your petal,
> furrows it with hard edge,
> like flint
> on a bright stone.

Now my ear, like the Sphinx's, may be heavy; such as it is, however, it can detect no essential difference between the unrhymed cadences of free verse and the unrhymed cadences of certain *modern* rhythmic prose. I emphasize "modern," because the rhythms of *vers libre* have little in common with the movement of the older prose.

Nor have they, indeed, any close affiliation with Whitman's verse. His elemental measures — "brawny enough, and limber and full enough," as he himself described them — breathe deep, whereas *vers libre* respires more lightly. The giant's swinging stride has passed, save for a lumbering Titan here and there; and like Agag, modern free verse walks delicately. It is rather the exquisite craftsmanship of France than the surging and orotund utterances of "Leaves of Grass" that has given to free verse, alike in England and America, its most distinctive qualities.

The rhythms of *vers libre* in English, then, unless I am mistaken, are in large degree the rhythms of a certain type of modern rhythmic prose. But that is not an assertion that free verse *is* prose. There are differences which set the one off from the other. The prose from which I have culled my excerpts does not maintain unbrokenly the rhythms which I have shown it to possess. If it did, we should certainly hesitate to call it prose. The best free verse poems, on the other hand, do maintain these rhythms consistently. And that is an important difference: the rhythms which are occasional in one are persistent in the other. Moreover, in prose like Meredith's and

Conrad's and Pater's and Hewlett's, the strophic element, the quality of return, although it is frequently present (as in most of the passages which I have quoted) is also not uniform. If it recurred with any regularity, the prose would at once become bad prose. On the other hand, it is the recurrence of "return" that makes verse verse at all. And my reason for declining, in spite of the evidence which I have pointed out, to ticket free verse as prose, is the fact that it deals with prose rhythms in a fashion which prose itself may not employ without thereby ceasing to be prose. That is as far as I can, at the moment, see my way. *Vers libre* is exploring the borderland between prose and verse. It is doing certain things which hitherto verse has done, and prose has not. It is doing certain other things which hitherto prose has done, and verse has not. It has simply staked out its claim in No Man's Land, and that is not a region mild, of calm and serene air. On the contrary, it is open to fire from two sides at once. And both sides are practicing their marksmanship. If free verse holds its ground (and from what I know of the versifiers I have a strong suspicion that it will), there will be at least an armistice by and by to consider terms.

As I see it, then — to anticipate that happy

hour — we are shut up to two alternatives.
Either we must declare that free verse is n't
verse, or our definition of verse must undergo
revision. The first is the simple and summary
way. The Queen in "Alice in Wonderland" is
a singularly appealing character, and "off with
his head" is a happy issue out of all our critical
afflictions. But it is the primrose path. And I fear
we must turn our eyes regretfully from this expeditious mode of settling criticism's business,
and choose the more thorny way. But it is also
too soon to reconstruct our definitions. Free
verse is not yet out of the experimental stage,
and the artists who practice it have still the
artisans in their own craft to reckon with. For
Browning's wish has at last come true:

> I want to know a butcher paints,
> A baker rhymes for his pursuit,
> Candlestick-maker much acquaints
> His soul with song.

The poetic world is already too safe for democracy. And the daily prayer of free verse should
be for deliverance from the tender mercies of
misguided friends. But when the air is clear,
and the fittest have survived, criticism can then
no longer evade the issue. Definitions follow
facts. If new facts are unmistakably established,

definitions must either be modified to fit them, or break down. There is no third alternative. The present movement wants its status determined in a moment. No one alive can possibly do that. If it has a fair field, it need ask no favor. It can make its contribution, and trust to time to assess its work and define its category. Meanwhile, let us meet a serious and sincere experiment in the technique of poetry with an open mind, and, without for a moment withholding criticism, let us at least criticise with understanding. Even the best of the group we are dealing with, run into absurdities; I am aware of few poets, even among the greatest, who have not. But no criticism which dwells on the extravagancies without at the same time recognizing the constructive attempt that lies behind them, is criticism worthy of the name.

Free verse, then, is an artistic medium of not yet fully developed possibilities. Its freedom is a liberty conditioned upon a subtle restriction of rhythms which it shares with prose, but which it wields in different fashion. It is gradually being perfected as an instrument of delicate precision and rare flexibility for recording the impressions of observed phenomena. Its danger lies in its very freedom, which, in the absence of a norm outside itself, permits form to become at times elusive. And being itself the child of a reaction, it foregoes, as a matter of conscience, certain possibilities, the abstention from which impoverishes it in one direction, while it is itself enriching poetry in another. In a word, just because the movement is a revolt, it is still too largely conditioned by its repugnances. That, as always, is a passing phase. It is more important to remember that the insurgents are also pioneers.

If free verse puts us to our shifts to place it, the so-called polyphonic prose comes near baffling the attempt. But where the poet dares to go, the critic must perforce gird up his loins and follow, envying, though he may not emulate the vigor and agility of his guides. One feels occasionally, however, like the worthy Bottom trying to keep up with Puck.

Polyphonic prose concerns us briefly here, because it is an endeavor, even more radical than *vers libre*, to combine the functions of both prose and verse. It was invented in France by M. Paul Fort; Miss Lowell was the first to attempt it in English; and she and Mr. John Gould Fletcher are its chief exponents in its adopted tongue. And since the new form is still in the plastic stage, I shall venture to point out quite frankly, but in no spirit of captious protest, wherein it seems to me to limit and even thwart its own possibilities. I realize my danger. A critic, who is at the same time friendly to the new and not blind to the defects of its virtues, is always in a parlous state. He can only ask that his intentions be taken as honorable, and pursue his way between the devil and the deep sea, where balance perilously resides, with such cheerfulness and resolution as he can muster.

What is polyphonic prose? It was heralded by Mr. Fletcher a couple of years ago as follows: "During the past year something has happened in the sphere of the arts quite as important in my opinion, as the European war in the sphere of politics . . . or the discovery of radium in that of science. A new poetic form, equal if not superior in value to *vers libre*, has made its appearance in English." That roars pretty loud, and thunders in the index, and I am deliberately quoting it, because it illustrates the sort of extreme that begets in retort the opposite extreme, and renders judicial criticism difficult. Mr. Fletcher defines polyphonic prose as a "way of fusing together unrhymed *vers libre* and rhymed metrical patterns, giving the rich decorative quality of the one and the powerful conciseness of statement of the other." "Intense and concise grasp of substance," he points out, "is not enough; the ear instinctively demands that this bare skeleton be clothed fittingly with all the beautiful and subtle orchestral qualities of assonance, alliteration, rhyme, and return." Free verse, that is, lacks something which regular verse has, notably "rhymed metrical patterns" and "orchestral qualities." I have said something to the same effect myself, you may remember, but I do not care to press the point. The new medium, then, is to combine in prose the merits of both sorts of verse. "Here," exclaims Mr. Fletcher, "are the Beethoven symphonies, the Bach fugues, the César Franck chorales, of poetry."

Miss Lowell's statement shuns flamboyancy, and is plain and definite.[1] "The word 'poly-

[1] For a still fuller discussion, printed since this paragraph was written, see the Preface to "Can Grande's Castle." And the achievement in "Can Grande's Castle" itself challenges, through its vividness and contagious zest in life and color, an unreluctant admiration. But the vividness and the zest are native to Miss Lowell, whatever the vehicle of their expression, and certain obstinate questionings of the medium, in two at least of its details, remain as intractable as Banquo's ghost. It is not, unless I am very much mistaken, the elements of rhyme and metre in "Can Grande's Castle" which give to it its rare union of vigor and deftness, precision and flexibility, imaginative grasp and clarity of detail. Its *formal* achievement lies rather, as I see it, in a remarkable extension of the potentialities latent in the movement of free verse. And

phonic' is [the] keynote of the genre." "'Polyphonic' means — many-voiced — and the form is so called because it makes use of all the 'voices' of poetry, viz., metre, *vers libre*, assonance, alliteration, rhyme, and return. It employs every form of rhythm, even prose rhythm at times, but usually holds no particular one for long. . . . The rhymes may come at the ends of the cadences, or may appear in close juxtaposition to each other, or may be only distantly related." So Miss Lowell, as over against Mr. Fletcher. The essential point, however, is the same. Polyphonic prose avails itself of the two qualities of regular verse which free verse rejects, namely metre and rhyme. It is an attempt at a single medium which shall gather into itself all the potentialities of prose, metre, unrhymed cadence, and rhyme. The enterprise is rather splendid in its audacity, and commands one's admiration, even when one doubts its entire feasibility. And despite ungrudging recognition of accomplishment, a lurking doubt persists.

For in my sober judgment such an attempt goes far towards marring one great medium of

these potentialities it might retain to the full (to venture once more my own opinion) without the adventitious aid of the two conventions which free verse rejects. In what follows, the grounds of this belief are given more at length.

expression in the effort to make it perform the functions of another. I am not forgetting that we have been warned against misunderstanding. "'Polyphonic prose' is not a prose form, although, being printed as prose, many people have found it difficult to understand this." But even an intelligent reader may be pardoned if he fails to understand that what is called prose and printed as prose is yet not prose. It is a little as if, your name being Schwarzkopf, and your physiognomy Teutonic, you should expect me to understand that you were Irish. I am not flippant, but genuinely anxious to make clear what seems to me to be the crucial point involved.

That point is this. The legitimate *expectation* with which we approach a given artistic medium is something that the artist is compelled to reckon with. We expect on the stage the make-up and the costumes which would disconcert us, if we met them on the street. *Per contra*, we should be thrown out of our reckoning, and disturbed in our enjoyment, if we saw on the stage faces without the heightening of make-up, and in unassisted light. Now in the same way we approach prose and verse respectively with perfectly definite and entirely different expectations. We rightly expect, when we approach verse, a heightening, both in form and in content; we look as a matter of course for rhyme, and assonance, and alliteration, and for cunningly fashioned rhythms and cadences, as we look on the stage for a corresponding heightening of effect. When we approach prose, on the other hand, we expect these things sparingly or not at all, precisely as we expect to find make-up on the faces of our friends either discreetly inconspicuous or absent altogether. And the artist in words, whether he will or no, faces as part of his problem the legitimate expectation with which his readers approach his medium.

Now I agree at once that polyphonic prose is not genuine prose. But it is called prose, and so printed. And it carries with it the *good-will*, so to speak, of prose. One cannot keep the form without assuming the responsibility of the form. And a prologue which says: "If you think I come here as a lion, it were pity of my life; no, I am no such thing," — such an assurance, except in a "Midsummer Night's Dream," does not quite meet the case. For when we find in that which bears the name and assumes the appearance of prose, the very things, rhyme and metre, which the masters of prose sweat to keep out of it, we are either confused or irritated, and sometimes both.

If it is felt that rhyme and metre must be kept, as essential and distinguishing elements of the medium, it is not, I think, straining a point to suggest that both the name and the printing of the new form be changed. The signals are set wrong, and the more intelligent the reader, the more violently he goes off the track.

But why, in sober sadness, should rhyme and metre be retained? All which has been urged against them by the adherents of free verse, applies with double force when they appear in a medium which carries with it the associations of prose. If rhyme and metre have no place in verse, they have, bull or no bull, less place there. And one is at once constrained to ask in addition: If they are effective in polyphonic prose, why do they cease to be effective when they appear in verse?

I know that polyphonic prose, if I may quote again, "usually holds no particular [rhythm] for long," and that it is printed as prose "for convenience, as it changes its character so often, with every wave of emotion, in fact." But it is precisely that constant shift of gear, so to speak, which disturbs us, and leaves us restless, rather than poised for flight. Either metre alone or free verse or prose alone is surely capable of keeping

pace with the varying shades of emotion. One
does n't, I think, *feel* at one instant metrically,
and unmetrically the next.

I am aware that all this sounds exceedingly
destructive. It is, however, neither destructive
nor hostile. If my criticism has any value at all,
that value is constructive. The medium has
shown itself capable, at its best, of splendid
vigor and vivid pictorial power, of richness of
color and sharpness of contrasts. It is a pity that
it should labor under a self-imposed handicap.
If rhyme and metre are abandoned, except in
intercalated passages, I suspect that the half
which is left will be more than the whole. In the
Preface to "Sword Blades and Poppy Seed" the
author remarked of the form we are discussing:
"Perhaps it is more suited to the French language than to English." The genius of the language is clearly one of the factors in the problem.
And there are obstacles in the way of such a
medium in English — among them what Keats
once called its "pouncing rhymes" — which do
not apply in French.

"Do not blame me," wrote Gray to Mason,
apropos of his insistence that "deigns" in a
poem of Mason's should be "deign'st" (even
though the change did wreck a rhyme!) — "do

not blame me, but the English tongue." And with fervent fellow-feeling I echo Gray.

May I add, as a matter of more than mere historical interest, that a very similar experiment was in full swing in Shakespeare's day? Lyly and the Euphuists were experimenting in artificial prose much as the polyphonists are to-day. And they too indulged in rhyme, and assonance, and balanced alliteration, and even metre: "The foule toad hath a faire stone in his head, the fine gold is found in the filthy earth"; "I will to Athens, there to tosse my bookes, no more in Naples to live with faire lookes"; "Then wounded with griefe, hee swounded with weaknesse"; "My tongue is too too base a Tryton to eternize her praise, that thus upholdeth our happy daies." Time fails for more than these shreds and patches. Euphuism ran its course and died, not without its contribution to the flexibility of the English tongue. The present experiment, which (despite its differences) is singularly like the old in many ways, may find perhaps in its extremes, if not a *caveat*, at least a caution.

Finally, so far as this phase of the subject is concerned, the attempt to efface the boundaries between prose and verse is symptomatic. It is only one aspect of the prevailing tendency to obliterate the dividing lines between all the arts. Music is trying to do the work of poetry and painting. Painting is striving to approximate on the one hand the rigidity of architecture, on the other the fluidity of music; poetry is experimenting with the technique of both, and it has cast besides an appropriating eye on the hardness and clarity of sculpture; while sculpture is meanwhile undergoing its own private metamorphosis. Kandinsky, says his English interpreter — and the same is asserted of Picasso and others by their followers — "Kandinsky is painting music; that is to say, he has broken down the barrier between music and painting." And Kandinsky's fundamental thesis is the encroachment of the arts upon one another. For him, "in music a light blue is like a flute, a darker blue a 'cello; a still darker a thunderous double bass; and the darkest blue of all an organ." One has only to think of Strauss, Debussy, Schönberg, and Stravinsky to recognize the converse tendency: the one group paints music, the other orchestrates painting. The phenomenon is nothing new. The reciprocal strivings of the arts to merge into each other is as old as art itself. Out of it will come, as there always has come in the past, a certain widening of the scope of each of the arts involved.

But with whatever augmented flexibility and enhanced expressiveness, it is more than probable that prose will remain prose, verse verse, music music, and color color, and that each will revert, with whatever gains, to its own technique. So far as poetry is concerned (unless the past can teach us nothing), it will lose little of value, and it may in the end gain more, from the present attempt to enlarge its possibilities.

Up to this point we have been dealing with the dubious borderland between prose and verse, and with recent adventures between the lines. The really serious incursions of prose upon poetry (not merely this time upon verse) have been, however, of a very different nature. So soon as we stop to think, it is clear that prose has preempted a lion's share of the territory once held, either in sovereignty or on equal terms, by poetry. The drama, save for a few gallant leaders of forlorn hopes, has surrendered unconditionally to prose. The epic (and largely the drama itself) has yielded place to the novel, and the briefer narrative in verse has retired before the ubiquitous short story. The conquered regions are firmly held and well administered, and it is useless to reargue a seemingly adjudicated case. I am not sure that poetry, without dispossessing prose, may not once more win a footing on equal terms in at least a portion of the abandoned field. The fact remains, however, that lyric and descriptive poetry are now all that hold their place unchallenged.

But even here there are signs of a confusion of aims which may work disaster. And this time the threatened encroachment of prose is along the road of content and not of form. With the range of poetry limited as it now is, how far afield may the poet go in his search for *themes?* Are there, in other words, subjects which are not adapted to poetry, but which rightly belong to prose? Are there limitations upon the poet's freedom of choice which are imposed, not by tradition, but by the very nature of his medium? That is a question of some importance, and the issue is far from being academic at the present moment.

The third article of the Imagists' Declaration of Principles is as follows: "To allow absolute freedom in the choice of subject." What that really means, I shall come to in a moment. What it means to the extremists is clear from one sentence in the summary of the aims of the French Paroxysmists: "It [that is, the movement known as "Paroxysm"] perceives the elements of poetry contained in modern cities, locomotives,

aeroplanes, dreadnaughts, and submarines; in a
stock exchange, a Wall Street, or a wheat pit;
and in every scientific marvel, and in the sonorous song of factories and railways." It is with
such pronunciamentos as that in mind, I suspect,
that the moderate Imagist declaration proceeds
to qualify its doctrine of absolute freedom. "It
is not good art," it continues, "to write badly
about aeroplanes and automobiles; nor is it necessarily bad art to write well about the past. We
believe passionately in the artistic value of modern life, but we wish to point out that there is
nothing so uninspiring nor so old-fashioned as an
aeroplane of the year 1911." And even the leader
of the English Vorticists remarks: "There is no
necessity to burn candles in front of your telephone apparatus or motor car." The issue, then,
is sharply joined between the two wings of the
Modernists themselves. And the question is one
of capital importance.

Let us strike at once to the heart of the matter.
What Thales and the Seven Sages thought and
wrote is matter of historical interest merely.
Sappho is contemporary with Rupert Brooke.
William Mason's "Ode to Mr. Pinchbeck on his
newly invented patent Candle Snuffers," published in the notable year of the Declaration of

Independence, is now introduced to you, I suspect, for the first time. It has followed its patent candle snuffers to oblivion. The contemporary "Elegy in a Country Churchyard" you know by heart; its theme is death, and death knows no oblivion. The themes of poetry are the enduring beliefs, and feelings, and passions of humanity, and everything whatsoever that is bound up with those. But life is endlessly taking on and sloughing off new shells, and collecting about it, only to discard them, its external, extrinsic paraphernalia and apparatus — its motor cars, and telephones, and submarines, and aeroplanes, and all the rest. Poetry has perfect freedom to concern itself with either. It may deal with what persists, and be understood, if it is good enough to last, a thousand years from now. It may lavish its art (as Tennyson did in a stanza which he did n't wait for time to kill) on the wonders of gas, and be rendered obsolete by electricity. It is perilous for poetry to be up to date.

Let us not, however, mistake the reasons. It is not tradition and convention that this time hold the flaming sword. It is an inhibition rather than a prohibition that interposes, and its roots are in part in the nature of poetry, and in part in the transiency of things. Until objects have become part and parcel of the loves, and hates, and hopes, and fears of men, they are not plastic stuff for art to work with. As objects, they are outside the domain of art. "It is poetry's job to catch up," says Mr. Ezra Pound, who was once a poet. Perhaps; but when poetry has caught up with a 1916 model, what doth it profit it in 1917? Things as things belong to prose. Even the purely intellectual is interwoven with poetry at the poet's risk. The sections of "In Memoriam" that deal with evolution were antiquated while Tennyson was yet alive; and the contemporary science in Dante, and Chaucer, and Ben Jonson, and Milton is a stone of stumbling and a rock of offence, except to those of us whom its elucidation helps to live. So long as a scientific textbook is obsolete in a decade or less, to poetize science is to court mortality. Wordsworth was absolutely right:

> The remotest discoveries of the Chemist, the Botanist, or Mineralogist, will be as proper objects of the poet's art as any upon which it can be employed, if the time should ever come when these things shall be . . . manifestly and palpably material to us as enjoying and suffering beings.

"Material to us as enjoying and suffering beings" — that is the clue through the labyrinth.

In that lies the reason why objects of immemorial use and wont have an initial advantage,
as themes for poetic treatment, over the new and
amazing machinery of modern life. That is why
an open road lends itself more readily to the
poet's purpose than a railway, a lamp than an
electrolier, an open fire than a radiator, a well
than a waterworks, a scythe than a McCormick
reaper. What I have said of words is true of
things. There are objects that are not in themselves more poetical than others, which yet,
through their associations, stir feeling more
directly. And these are perennial in their
appeal.

But once more it is with things as it is with
words. If the creative energy is strong enough,
the most intractable words may be merged, as
we have seen, in the very stuff of poetry. And if
imagination, instead of being caught in wheels
and pistons, penetrates to whatever of human —
glory of motion, daring of flight, beauty and
terror and power — is bound up with invention
and the processes of modern life, then aeroplanes,
and railways, and wireless telegraphy, and all the
rest become fit matter for its exercise. And the
poet is by ancient right the interpreter of their
significance. But he dare not concern himself

with how the wheels go round. That is the privilege of prose. Eighteenth-century poetry usurped the prerogatives of prose at just this point, and its *débâcle* offers food for thought, as poetry stands again at the dividing of the ways. I wish I might fill the next few pages with copious extracts from King's "Art of Cookery," and Garth's "Dispensary," and Grainger's "Sugar-Cane," and Dyer's "Fleece," and Thomson's "Sickness," and Green's "The Spleen," and Dodsley's "Agriculture," and Armstrong's "Art of Preserving Health," and Glover's "London, or the Progress of Commerce," and a few other like attempts to wring poetry out of the stuff of prose. Here, instead, is a part of the Argument to the third book of "The Sugar-Cane":

"Hymn to the month of January, when crop begins. Address. Planters have employment all the year round. Planters should be pious. . . . Crop begun. Cane-cutting described. Effects of music. Great care requisite in feeding the mill. Humanity towards the maimed recommended. . . . How to preserve the laths and mill-points from sudden squalls. Address to the Sun, and praise of Antigua. A cattle-mill described. Care of mules. Diseases to which they are subject. . . . The necessity of a strong clear fire, in boiling. Planters should always have a spare set of vessels, because the iron furnaces are apt to crack, and copper vessels to melt. The danger of throwing cold water into a thorough-heated furnace. Cleanliness and skimming well recommended."

Reminding you that this is part of the prospectus of a *poem*, I shall come to the description of the mill. And this is not the prospectus, but the poem itself. Remember, please, that Grainger's theme is to his day what the aeroplane, and the locomotive, and the automobile are to ours.

> By transverse beams
> Secure the whole; and in the pillar'd frame,
> Sink, artist, the vast bridge-tree's mortise'd form
> Of pond'rous hiccory; hiccory time defies:
> To this be nail'd three polish'd iron plates;
> Whereon, three steel capouces, turn with ease,
> Of three long rollers, twice-nine inches round,
> With iron cas'd, and jagg'd with many a cogg.
> The central cylinder exceeds the rest
> In portly size, thence aptly captain nam'd.
> To this be rivetted th' extended sweeps;
> And harness to each sweep two seasoned mules:
> They pacing round, give motion to the whole.
> The close-brac'd cylinders with ease revolve
> On their greas'd axle; and with ease reduce
> To trash the canes thy Negroes throw between.
> Fast flows the liquor through the lead-lin'd spouts;
> And depurated by opposing wires,
> In the receiver floats a limpid stream.

That is what happens when poetry usurps the place of prose, and meddles with machinery. One is impelled to urge upon the Muse the heartfelt caution which Grainger offers to his planter:

O beware!
Nor trust, between the steel-cas'd cylinders,
The hand incautious: off the member snapt
Thou'lt ever rue; sad spectacle of woe!

Let me set over against that a poem which is
not great, but which offers an illuminating con-
trast — Charles Tennyson-Turner's sonnet on
the "Steam Threshing-Machine with the Straw-
Carrier":

Flush with the pond the lurid furnace burn'd
At eve, while smoke and vapour fill'd the yard;
The gloomy winter sky was dimly starr'd,
The fly-wheel with a mellow murmur turn'd;

While, ever rising on its mystic stair
In the dim light, from secret chambers borne,
The straw of harvest, sever'd from the corn,
Climb'd, and fell over, in the murky air.

I thought of mind and matter, will and law,
And then of him, who set his stately seal
Of Roman words on all the forms he saw
Of old-world husbandry: *I* could but feel
With what a rich precision *he* would draw
The endless ladder, and the booming wheel!

I have quoted that partly for its own sake — for
its fusion of pictorial power and imaginative suggestion; partly for the sake of its reference to the
"Georgics." For in the "Georgics," Virgil has
dealt with implements and utensils in the one

and only way open to poetry in making its own the machinery that has taken their place. He has given the essence and not the accident; he has never lost sight of pictorial beauty, nor relaxed precision where precision was required; and he has imbued every object that he touches, with the light and warmth and color absorbed from its contact with life. And modern poetry may still gain hints for its craft in the exactness of impression and the imaginative vision of the "Georgics."

There is still another caution which it is well to keep in mind. It is in its dealings with the sharply impinging actualities of contemporary life that poetry is apt to forget that art is fundamentally illusion. "*It is too true*," wrote Flaubert of his "Éducation Sentimentale," "and speaking æsthetically it lacks the falsehood of perspective." Walt Whitman, for example, was constantly "too true," and some of his successors follow in his steps. "Strange and hard that paradox true I give," he writes, in "A Song for Occupations"; "objects gross and the unseen soul are one." That is a good beginning, but here is how he proceeds:

House-building, measuring, sawing the boards,
Blacksmithing, glass-blowing, nail-making, coopering, tin-roofing, shingle-dressing,

Ship-joining, dock-building, fish-curing, flagging of side-
    walks by flaggers,
The pump, the pile-driver, the great derrick, the coal-
    kiln and brick-kiln —

and on through more than a full page of catalogue, including:

Beef on the butcher's stall, the slaughter-house of the
    butcher, the butcher in his killing clothes,
The pens of live pork, the killing-hammer, the hog-
    hook, the scalder's tub, gutting, the cutter's
    cleaver, the packer's maul, and the plenteous
    winterwork of pork-packing.

And then he concludes:

These shows all near you by day and night — work-
    men! whoever you are, your daily life! . . .
In them realities for you and me, in them poems for
    you and me . . .
In them the development good — in them all themes,
    hints, possibilities.

Nothing could be more profoundly true than
that. *In* things are poems and possibilities, but
the things themselves are neither. I believe that
poetry has a great and supremely difficult adventure before it, in the interpretation of the life
immediately about it, with the complex and tyr-
annous machinery in which it is involved. The
poets recognize to the full the greatness of the
task; its almost insurmountable difficulties they

are taking lightly. There are essays in the right direction. Poetry wants even Chicago, and Carl Sandburg, in a poem that is like the blow of a fist in the face, gives it to us. I do not like poems that black your eye, any more than Professor Firkins likes poems that put up their mouth to be kissed. But Chicago is not an unobtrusive town, and Mr. Sandburg has at least tried to grasp it, and hurl a complete impression at us. And that is something.

In a word, the passionate belief of modern poetry in the artistic value of modern life is not misplaced. But it must catch the permanent behind the modern, for while the poet writes, the modern is slipping into obsolescence, and hardening into the rigid Past.

The defection to prose of the larger forms of poetry has had another result. The short has tended to become the fragmentary. That, of course, does not inevitably follow. And we may consider for a moment the general shift of taste from long to short.

The Middle Ages liked things long. "I thank you," writes the lover to his lady in Machaut's "Voir-dit," "that the length of what I write does n't bore you, for certainly when I begin, I don't know how to end." And Peronne was a true child of her time, as well as a courteous lady, when she replied in her next letter: "By my faith, if what you wrote stretched out as long as the 'Romance of the Rose' or the 'Lancelot,' it would not bore me in the least." Now the "Romance of the Rose" reached 22,814 lines, and there is one version of the "Lancelot" of which the fragment that survives extends beyond its forty-seven thousandth line! Nor must we forget the account which Froissart gives in "Le Dit dou Florin" of how in the winter of 1388, night after night, in rain or wind, he went from his inn to the castle of Gaston Phébus, Count of Foix, and there in the brightly lighted room where supper was spread, read aloud, night after night, for ten mortal weeks, six before Christmas and four after, his own interminable romance, the "Méli-ador." And Gaston Phébus — witness his treatment of his little son — was not a naturally patient person. One recalls, moreover, that Deschamps had begun on the thirteenth thousand of his lines on marriage when death stayed his hand.

Of course our less remote ancestors are a close second in endurance. The ten volumes of Mlle. de Scudéry's "Le Grand Cyrus" ran to 6679 pages, and the rest of the heroic romances kept

the same leisurely pace — a pace successfully
emulated by "Clarissa Harlowe" and "Sir
Charles Grandison." Tennyson, who liked what
he called "those great still books," used to say,
"I wish there were a great novel in hundreds of
volumes, that I might go on and on"; but he
would have found few, I fear, to concur in his
longing. The ten-volume novel shrank to three;
the three to one; even on that the short story is
rapidly encroaching; and the ten-word headline
bids fair to become the type of modern narrative.
The old-fashioned, far-flung epic simile has given
place to the concision and compactness of the
metaphor. And poetry itself, in an age of efficiency, must go through no unnecessary motions.
The tired business man — Mr. Wells's "weary
Titan" — wants his poems snapped at him,
rapped at him, barked at him, like the pregnant
utterances of the heroes of the detective stories.

Now in the hands of an artist, a poem of a
dozen or sixteen lines may have as flawless unity
as an epic, and the emphasis upon compression,
and concentration, and "quintessentializing," together with the weight attached to the strophic
element in verse, makes indubitably for unity of
form. But the poets, now as always, are hopelessly outnumbered by the poetasters. And since

it is as easy to write verse (especially free verse) badly, as it is difficult to write it well, the total impression of recent poetry is apt to be that of a thing of shreds and patches.

For the great danger ahead of poetry, when it is primarily interested in the recording of sensuous impressions, is that it cease to *think*. I trust I have made it clear that I should regard poetry which embodied thought alone, as prose in the disguise of verse. But however feeling may render plastic the stuff of poetry, the poem, if it be worthy of the name, is forged in the brain. What I feel about the ruck of recent verse, especially as it ebbs and flows by the moon through the monthly periodicals, is that its writers have thought nothing through, and least of all a poem. I could read you by the score, from the mass of recent verse, impressions, often beautifully phrased, which as poems have neither beginning nor middle nor end. If one could but feel that they were preliminary studies, like Rembrandt's or Leonardo's sketches, one might gladly rest content. But they are not. They are fondly regarded as finished works themselves. And so we get the *disjecti membra poetæ* — as if the poet had been hit and scattered into crystal fragments by a bomb, or had been, at best, cut up, like Romeo, into little stars. Except in some of the more serious craftsmen, the architectonic power has suffered atrophy. In the great poets, impressions are richly present, but they are integral components of a whole, fused from innumerable parts by the steady, unintermitted energy of the creative imagination. It is that sustained, fusing energy of which, I think, we feel the lack to-day — and not in poetry only. It is not mere accident that much modern verse is cinematographic. The trend of all but the best current poetry is away from the consecutive and towards the discrete. I have read volumes of recent verse in which little fragment after little fragment is dropped into the receptive mind, as the successive globules, when a faucet is turned off, fall with distinct yet gentle impact upon the water in a bowl. And one cries to Heaven, after an hour of it, for the sweep of the winds, and the heaving of the tides, and even shattering cataracts of rain. One wearies quickly of what somebody has called "thumb-nail sketches of the star in the puddle."

I wish again to say distinctly that this indictment does not lie against all recent poetry. But it does grow in large measure, I believe, out of the quest for externality and immediacy of impression. The stronger spirits are able to impose their will upon the phantasmagoria of images which they evoke. The others shed impressions as a cat sheds hairs.

Is poetry, then, going to the wall? Far from it, I should say. Since we happen at the present moment to be alive, however, we get the bad contemporary verse together with the good. And since quantitatively the bad is in excess, the effect is rather overwhelming. What we overlook is the fact that every previous generation has gone through the same experience. The only difference is that their bad verse is safely dead and decently interred. Ours is n't — yet! By and by it will be, and the happy lecturer a hundred years from now will find the house swept and garnished, and will have the simple task of discoursing on the early-twentieth-century classics. But I shall not anticipate his list!

VIII

I HAVE said "Anglo-Saxon," because there is no other term that quite expresses what I have in mind. And "Anglo-Saxon" is itself ambiguous. By the Anglo-Saxon tradition I mean the ideals and qualities that have been handed down through those who speak the tongue that Shakespeare spoke — the poetic tradition of our English-speaking race. It is a very splendid tradition. And it has both the surpassing merits and the complementary defects of the breed from which it springs. I shall not attempt to deal with it exhaustively. But in these days when the whole of Wordsworth's line is true as it was never true before: "We must be free or die, who speak the tongue That Shakespeare spake" — in these days we turn back to our kind, merits and defects alike, with new affection and a great pride. And I am allowing myself in closing to say certain things I want to say, without particular regard to their connection with either convention or revolt.

There are two outstanding facts about the

English language which have their counterparts
in English poetry. In each there is the directness
and the virility of the native stock; in each the
flexibility that comes from an unrivalled power
of assimilation. But through all the influences
and agencies from without, in speech and poetry
alike, the stock persists; and be the influence
French, or Italian, or Spanish, or what not, the
resultant is none of these, but English. It is this
persistent native strain, with all its imperfections
on its head, to which we may now come.

Let me illustrate the qualities that I have
particularly in mind. Here is a paragraph from
Malory's "Morte Darthur":

And as the king lay in his cabin in the ship, he fell
in a slumbering, and dreamed a marvellous dream:
him seemed that a dreadful dragon did drown much of
his people, and he came flying out of the west, and
his head was enamelled with azure, and his shoulders
shone as gold, his belly like mails of a marvellous hue,
his tail full of tatters, his feet full of fine sable, and his
claws like fine gold; and an hideous flame of fire flew
out of his mouth, like as the land and water had flamed
all of fire. After him seemed there came out of the orient
a grimly boar all black in a cloud, and his paws as big
as a post; he was rugged looking roughly, he was the
foulest beast that ever man saw, he roared and romed
so hideously that it were marvel to hear. Then the
dreadful dragon advanced him, and came in the wind
like a falcon, giving great strokes on the boar, and the

boar hit him again with his grisly tusks that his breast was all bloody, and that the hot blood made all the sea red of his blood. Then the dragon flew away all on an height, and came down with such a swough, and smote the boar on the ridge, which was ten foot large from the head to the tail, and smote the boar all to powder, both flesh and bones, that it flittered all abroad on the sea.

There is in the diction of that sinewy prose a directness, a vigor, a forthrightness, which are a part of our ancestral heritage. They are part of our ancestral heritage in poetry as well.

For from "Beowulf" down to the "Barrack-Room Ballads" a splendidly robust and virile strain has run through English poetry. Think of a few of the many names: "Beowulf" itself, the Romances and the Ballads, the "Canterbury Tales," "Gammer Gurton's Needle," first and second "Henry IV," Ben Jonson's comedies, Dryden's satires, "Tam o'Shanter" and the "Jolly Beggars," "Don Juan," the "Biglow Papers," "Leaves of Grass." Common to all of them, despite their infinite array of differences, is a masculine energy that never overlooks the mass in the detail. Ornament, prettiness, finesse are secondary qualities; boldness of conception, frankness of delineation, directness of speech are their distinctive marks. They are less concerned with moonlight and with skylarks and

with enamels and cameos, than with men and
their affairs. They deal with action rather than
with objects; they are dynamic rather than static; they do not leave the brain idle while they
seek to touch the heart, or titillate the sense.
The poets whom I have particularly in mind —
Chaucer, Ben Jonson, Dryden, Samuel Johnson,
Burns, Scott, Byron, Henley, and their line —
looked on life as what we call nowadays "a man's
job," and they looked with masculine eyes. That
implies limitations without doubt. The qualities
that we name feminine are apt to be present in
fusion with the so-called masculine in all the
greatest art. And exquisiteness, and delicacy,
and charm go hand in hand with vigor, and raci-
ness, and even coarseness in some of the poets
whom I have named. The two points on which
I am intent are these: the English tradition includes a magnificently virile strain; and that
strain shows itself chiefly in poetry that takes
for its province the actions of men.

Let me say at once that it is not a question
of admiring either robustness or delicacy to the
exclusion of the other. It is not even a matter
of being happy with either, were tother away.
Catholicity of taste is still, even in these days of
partisan politics in poetry, at once desirable and

possible. If I say that I like one thing, it is bad
logic, however usual, to fling it in my face that I
must therefore dislike the opposite. And particularly in the case of the antithesis we are considering, there is danger of misunderstanding. I
like tremendously, for instance, this drinking-
song from "Gammer Gurton's Needle":

> I cannot eat but little meat,
>   My stomach is not good;
> But sure I think that I can drink
>   With him that wears a hood.
> Though I go bare, take ye no care,
>   I nothing am a-cold;
> I stuff my skin so full within
>   Of jolly good ale and old.
>   Back and side go bare, go bare;
>   Both foot and hand go cold;
>   But, belly, God send thee good ale enough,
>   Whether it be new or old. . . .
>
> And Tib, my wife, that as her life
>   Loveth well good ale to seek,
> Full oft drinks she till ye may see
>   The tears run down her cheek:
> Then doth she trowl to me the bowl
>   Even as a maltworm should,
> And saith, "Sweetheart, I took my part
>   Of this jolly good ale and old.". . .

That is neither delicate, nor exquisite, nor re-
fined. But my liking for it does not in the least
detract from my delight in this:

> Drink to me only with thine eyes,
>   And I will pledge with mine;
> Or leave a kiss but in the cup,
>   And I'll not look for wine.
> The thirst that from the soul doth rise
>   Doth ask a drink divine;
> But might I of Jove's nectar sup,
>   I would not change for thine.

The thing we may regret is that the masculine vigor of the one is somewhat in abeyance in English poetry to-day. `

I suspect that is due in part to a fact which has met us elsewhere. Prose has taken over, in the drama, and the novel, and the short story, that portion of the field of poetry which once claimed as its own men and action and affairs. The tradition has not lapsed; it has been diverted from poetry to prose. And however great the gain for the one, the loss has been indubitable for the other. I suppose that if Chaucer had lived to-day, he would have written prose fiction. If he had, many a brow would now be looking to its laurels. Nevertheless, literature would probably have been on the whole the poorer. For the form of the "Canterbury Tales" has given them an immortality which prose could scarcely confer — precisely as the swiftness and vividness and verve of "Tam o'Shanter" find their inevitable vehicle in verse. Poetry, in a word, has abandoned far too lightly the play for the setting. The play is still the thing. "Scenery is fine," wrote Keats, whose letters I am quoting freely, "but human nature is finer — the sward is richer for the tread of a . . . nervous English foot — the Eagle's nest is finer, for the Mountaineer has looked into it." And in the midst of the finesse, and the artistry, and the meticulous minutiæ of recent verse, one longs at times, not for less refinement but for more virility, for a return on the part of poetry, without the relinquishment of the impressions of things, to the doings of men.

I believe the wind sits in the shoulder of the sail and convoy is assistant, for the adventurous voyager who will sail the old lanes of the seas again. Whatever one's fears and scruples about polyphonic prose, of one thing there can be no doubt: it is at least striking, definitely and with something of the old-time directness, into the open road of narrative. I am not one of the devotees of the "Spoon River Anthology." It lacks, in my judgment, the distinction which would lift it to the level of great art. Yet it too is in the line of the great tradition, in its immediate and sole concern with life. And its chief significance lies in its amazing popularity — a vogue which means, unless I am much mistaken, that the readers of poetry are ready, even eager, to welcome once more in verse the actions and the lives of men. That is, and always has been, and presumably will always be, the deepest and most abiding human interest. And if ever a time was ripe for its return, that time is now.

Let us look at another closely related element of the tradition. English poetry has been in large measure a poetry of *ideas*, and that has been both its glory and, on occasion, its undoing.

It has been its glory, because the great poets have always recognized that we do not cease to think, even when we also feel profoundly, or exert imaginative energy. There is, to be sure, a fantastic notion abroad these days that thought, whatever other excellence it may possess, is not a thing of beauty, and therefore is taboo for poetry. Now I grant at once that poetry's first concern, yesterday, to-day, and *in secula seculorum*, is beauty. And pure ratiocination, where the intellect works cold and aloof in dry light, whatever may be its austere and remote beauty of another sort, is not as such the stuff of poetry. Its *results* may be; its own fit medium of expression, as unaccommodated thought, is prose. But if thought, however penetrating or profound, takes body in beauty of imperishable *form*, even a poet may with impunity plead guilty to its exercise. "I hope," wrote Keats the year before his death, "I hope I am a little more of a Philosopher than I was, consequently a little less of a versifying Pet-lamb." We may continue without compunction to look askance at detachable gems of thought in verse. But we do not, I think, find either the "Divine Comedy," or "Hamlet," or "Faust" the less poetry, because we never exhaust the creative energy of thought that they hold stored to quicken thought, whenever there is vital contact with a mind.

But that quickening power, let me repeat, is exercised through something more than thought, as such. Dante thought profoundly in the "Convivio," and Goethe (however wrongly) in the "Farbenlehre." And we think after them when we read these things. More than that happens, when we read the "Divine Comedy" and "Faust." We are not merely thinking after them; we are started on voyages of our own. There is something that eludes analysis, but which is the very heart of poetry, in the mysterious fusion of thought and form in supremely great verse. Take these lines from "Antony and Cleopatra":

Cheer your heart.
Be you not troubled with the time, which drives
O'er your content these strong necessities;
But let determin'd things to destiny
Hold unbewail'd their way.

"The time, *which drives O'er your content these
strong necessities*" — there in one phrase is the
burden of this tragic year of our Lord, which has
just dawned upon the planet.[1] And in the rest of
it: "But let determin'd things to destiny Hold
unbewail'd their way" — is not only the spirit of
"what's brave, what's noble, Let's do it after
the high Roman fashion," but, stern and austere
in its simplicity, the ultimate formulation of the
spirit with which, by millions, the supreme tragedy is being met to-day. And I submit that a
thought so imperishably phrased that it sums up
not only the cataclysm of a world, but also the
stoic and indomitable temper that endures it, is
of at least as much worth as the embodiment of
a sensuous impression, however exquisite. That
has its place, and it is high, but it is not the solitary peak of poetry.

The poet, then, cannot think too deeply, if he
thinks through the imagination, which gives to
thought its wings. Without that, ideas *are* out of

[1] I have allowed these lines to stand as they were written in
January, 1918.

place in poetry. With it, no idea, however freighted with pabulum for the brain, is alien or inimical to poetry. That means that when a poet thinks, he must think as a poet. If he thinks as a Presbyterian, or a professor, or a socialist, or a partisan of any movement, or an adherent of any creed, he comes under Touchstone's anathema — he is damn'd, like an ill-roasted egg all on one side. He is versifying his ideas, such as they are, not impregnating thought with imaginative beauty — which is one at least of poetry's high prerogatives.

It happens to be my business to teach English literature. That carries with it for any frail mortal a lurking peril. There develops, insidiously and unawares, the academic bent of mind — an excellent thing in its place, but devastating out of it. But in spite of shades of the prison-house, some of us still read poetry as human beings, and it is as a human being, so far as possible, that I am speaking now. And most of us, I believe, find satisfaction in the challenge to thought, while at the same time we feel, and, through an awakened imagination, see. And poetry at its greatest seeks for nothing less than the whole of us. There is, I know, a public that does n't want to think. But if, through poetry, its brain is surreptitiously reached, at least it does n't know it 's hurt, and it even may and sometimes does experience a new delight in the unasked for and involuntary exercise of its intelligence. And anyway, neither they nor we get all of what a great poem has to give. For when thought invests itself in imaginative beauty, it becomes, by the miracle which we call genius, inexhaustible.

Now the great tradition in poetry has always offered ungrudging hospitality to ideas, and that, as I have said, has been one of its glories. It has been more than once its evil genius, too. For the intellectual element in poetry must be completely permeated with imagination and fused with feeling, if it is not to mar where it should make. And that supreme and difficult interpenetration has by no means always been achieved. Much of the work of some of the greatest has been vitiated by thinking, unassimilated to the inexorable demands of art. I shall not reiterate what has been said a hundred times about Donne, and Wordsworth, and Browning, and Shelley, and Meredith, for example — five shining and imperishable names. Each, in his way, exemplifies the peril that besets a highly gifted poetic nature, when at bad moments thought inhibits imagination, instead of being transfused and informed and made luminous by it. Even Shelley sometimes mingles poetry and propaganda to their mutual disaster. And though Dryden's intellectual vigor and Pope's consummate art raised at times that shibboleth of the eighteenth century, the understanding, almost to the level of imagination, in the verse of their school it persisted flinty and intractable.

Let us not, however, confuse the issue. Merely to think is itself no easy task, as most of us know to our sorrow. To think imaginatively is the gift of genius. To give to thought, winged with imagination, an imperishable *form* — that is the supreme achievement of genius in its highest exercise. And the fact that even genius has sometimes lapsed, and the further fact, sad but inexorable, that the vast majority of those who write verse are unendowed with the assimilating alchemy of genius — these facts should not betray us into the repudiation of a great tradition.

We are dealing with a phase of the subject which requires endless qualification, because the intellectual element runs through poetry like a great watershed. On the one side the streams flow off toward the sublime; on the other they plunge headlong to the ridiculous; and the turn of a hair may save or damn. And the Eng-

lish tradition has steered a course not without
lapses down the wrong side of the ridge, with
respect to one vitally important matter. Is it
poetry's business to *teach* ? There is perhaps no
single interrogation which sets so swiftly the
storm signals flying. And there is probably no
answer which will command universal assent.
The poetic tradition is itself ambiguous, but we
can at least discriminate.

There is native to our Anglo-Saxon blood a
distinctly didactic, even homiletic, strain. Coleridge once said to Lamb, "I believe, Charles,
you never heard me preach." "My dear fellow,"
replied Lamb, "I never heard you do anything
else." And it is one of our racial traits to point a
moral even while we adorn a tale.

> O Reader! hast thou ever stood to see
> > The Holly Tree?
> The eye that contemplates it well perceives
> > Its glossy leaves
> Order'd by an intelligence so wise
> As might confound the Atheist's sophistries.

> I love to view these things with curious eyes,
> > And moralise:
> And in this wisdom of the Holly Tree
> > Can emblems see
> Wherewith perchance to make a pleasant rhyme,
> One which may profit in the after time.

I shall not quote the rest of the poem, in which Southey asseverates that

> Gentle at home amid [his] friends [he'd] be
> Like the high leaves upon the Holly Tree,

and expresses the pious hope that

> In [his] age as cheerful [he] might be
> As the green winter of the Holly Tree.

Dorothy Wordsworth's birch tree, "glancing in the wind like a flying sunshiny shower," and "bending to the breezes as if for the love of its own delightful motions" is worth unnumbered cords sawed from Southey's holly tree. For there are tongues in trees assuredly, but they are the tongues of trees, and not of tractates.

Coleridge reports in his "Table Talk" a conversation between himself and Mrs. Anna Letitia Barbauld—who wrote, among other things, "An Address to the Deity," and "Hymns in Prose for Children." "Mrs. Barbauld," says Coleridge, "once told me that she admired the 'Ancient Mariner' very much, but that there were two faults in it, — it was improbable, and had no moral. As for the probability, I owned that that might admit some question; but as to the want of a moral, I told her that in my own judgment the poem had too much; and that the only, or

chief fault, if I might say so, was the obtrusion of
the moral sentiment so openly on the reader as
a principle or cause of action in a work of such
pure imagination. It ought to have had no more
moral than the Arabian Nights' tale of the merchant's sitting down to eat dates by the side of
a well, and throwing the shells aside, and lo! a
genie starts up, and says he *must* kill the afore-
said merchant, *because* one of the date shells had,
it seems, put out the eye of the genie's son."

It was Coleridge rather than Mrs. Barbauld
who was right. Yet even here we must discriminate. For the poem offers a striking example of
ethical values employed both as art may, and
also as art may not, employ them. The "Ancient
Mariner," to a degree surpassed in the case of
few other poems in English, is a work of sheer
imagination. It is absolutely in keeping with that
fact that it should have a firm yet flexible framework. And it has. It is not inconsistent with its
imaginative quality that the framework, if one
plots it, looks like the bare bones of a sermon —
Crime; Punishment: (a) for oneself, (b) for the
innocent; Penitence, and the Burden falls; Penance; Absolution; The Penance of Life. But one
does n't plot it, unless one is out (as I am at the
moment) for that sort of game. As one reads the

poem, its skeleton is as unobtrusive as yours or
mine; as Hazlitt says of the allegory in the
"Faëry Queene," it does n't bite. And what I
wish to emphasize is the fact that, *as Coleridge
employs it*, it has a high artistic and imaginative
function. The sense of the homely and traditional
moral values is to the poem — like the quiet
harbor and the wedding feast — part of "the
known and familiar landscape," to quote Coleridge's famous statement, over which the sudden
charm of the accidents of light and shade is
to be diffused. For there is, in fact, nothing so
strange as the familiar, when a cataclysm has
changed *you*, and left *it* untouched. The ethical
background of the poem, then, is not a moral; it
is an imaginative use of moral values, as an integral element of an imaginative conception —
and that is a horse of a totally different color. It
is when, at the close of the poem, an explicit
moral is definitely drawn (how under heaven
Mrs. Barbauld missed it, I don't know) that the
moral sentiment is, as Coleridge says, obtruded
openly on the reader. The "Ancient Mariner"
ought to be as bare of a categorically pointed
moral as "Kubla Khan."

Poetry may teach, then, if it teaches in art's
way — if, in Browning's phrase, it "does the

thing shall breed the thought." "To instruct delightfully," says Dryden, following Sir Philip Sydney, "is the general end of all poetry. Philosophy instructs, but it performs its work by precept, which is not delightful, or not so delightful as example." Browning and Dryden are at one; the poet's business is not with precept. The teacher's and the preacher's is — though not so much, I shrewdly suspect, as they suppose. Poetry does not teach us, but it allows us to be taught, as life and the universe permit us, if we will, to learn. The poet's sense of ethical values, if he has it, may communicate itself to us, as Shakespeare's does, implicitly, without the intrusion of a moral sentiment. "We hate poetry," wrote Keats, "that has a palpable design upon us. . . . Poetry should be great and unobtrusive," he goes on, "a thing which enters into one's soul, and does not startle it or amaze it with itself — but with its subject." So soon as he moralizes, the poet has abdicated his throne.

Once more, the end of art is the disclosure of beauty. But the great tradition of English poetry is sound in its steadfast insistence that beauty is latent in actions and ideas, and may be present even when actions and ideas have ethical quality. I believe profoundly in the doctrine of art for art's sake—of art, that is, for the sake of what art alone can give, and give only in art's way. That, as I see it, admits no alternative. But I object to the limitation of the dictum to anything short of beauty wherever it is latent, and awaiting the touch of art to release it and reveal it. That means that I accept as valid, so far as it goes, the *Symbolistes'* application of the shibboleth, and its rejuvenation by their present-day disciples. But the formula imposes fetters upon art, when it confuses art's *way*, which is immutable, with the *themes* of art, which are subject to no limitation save their fitness for endowment with artistic form. And a theme that possesses ethical implications, so treated as to disclose beauty, fulfils the stern requirements of *l'art pour l'art* as completely as a similar treatment of themes that may be fitly described as *Emaux et Camées*. The sole criterion is the treatment. If the poet remains relentlessly the artist, he is as true to art for art's sake when he composes an "Ode to Duty," as when he writes a "Symphonie en Blanc Majeur." The one inexorable mandate is that he take art's way.

It is when art's way is abandoned, and only then, that poetry is overtaken by disaster. And that, and that alone, is why the Anglo-Saxon tradition, with its emphasis on content, has too often led its followers astray. Didacticism in poetry is high seriousness turned wrong side out. And what one gets as a result is suggestive of Stevenson's malign but alluring reference to George Eliot as "a high, but (may we not add?) a rather dry lady." Nor is it, perhaps, without significance that most of the poets who have thus offended have been, in varying degrees, devoid of humor. For didacticism and a sense of humor are mutually exclusive qualities. And that suggests the saving grace.

For through the high gift of humor and the resultant power of detachment, English poetry has been enriched with a long series of magnificently unmoral embodiments of moral reprehensibility. I decline, respectfully but firmly, to split hairs over the question of casuistry involved in that deliberate paradox. What I wish to say is this. Any poetic tradition is fairly secure, in the final audit, against the charge of surrender to the didactic, which can set over against the worst that Southey, and Wordsworth, and Martin Tupper, and Felicia Hemans at their worst can do, the Pandar of "Troilus and Creseyde," and the Wife of Bath and all the engaging rascals of the "Canterbury Tales," and Falstaff, and Cleopatra, and

Tam o'Shanter, and the Jolly Beggars, and Don Juan, and Fra Lippo Lippi. They might not save Sodom and Gomorrah, but they insure English tradition against possession in fee simple by the Philistines. For English poetry, whatever its defections into the parochial, has also gloriously recognized the truth which Goethe once stated in speaking of Byron. The excellent Eckermann had expressed a doubt regarding Byron's value as a moral factor in the uplifting of humanity. "I must take issue with you," said Goethe, "Byron's daring, dash, and grandiosity — has that not formative value? We must guard," he went on, "against seeking such values only in what is distinctly pure and moral. *Alles grosse bildet*, — whatever is great is creative." That from the creator of Mephistopheles has weight. And even the Puritan Milton — Heaven be thanked for it! — rose to the highest height of his great argument in the superb conception of the moral grandeur of Satan.

There is another tendency that demands a passing word. It does not belong to the great tradition, but, at least since the days of Laurence Sterne, it has flowed, warm, and moist, and saccharine, and sometimes nebulously ecstatic, through minor English verse, and occasionally a major poet relaxes his fibre and admits it. For English poetry — and here alas! it cannot throw stones from its glass house at Germany — is sometimes sentimental. One of the most delectable articles I know is a paper in the "Essays and Studies" by members of the English Association, entitled "Some Suggestions about Bad Poetry." I commend it to the Imagists as an arsenal of weapons, and to the non-combatant reader as a Pill to Purge Melancholy. Now sentimentality is at its worst in verse, when emotion flows over a theme, vague, and hazy, and amorphous, with the non-inebriating quality of warm tea. It is the sort of thing that in its earlier days revelled (as Miss Sichel notes in the article referred to) in "Lines to Cherokees," and "Odes on the Sentiments of Young Indians at Sunrise." "There is nothing," she proceeds, "that cannot be imagined by people of no imagination, and the emotions of colored races on large natural phenomena admit of any amount of woolly thoughts, facile emotions, and false possibilities. Perhaps," she continues, "this is the reason why this era can boast more minor poetesses than any other." If the thing were confined to musings on the emotional reactions of the untutored but sensitive savage, it would not be so bad. But nothing evades the sentimentalist. Some of you, I hope, remember the heroine of Mrs. Radcliffe's "Romance of the Forest." May I refresh your memory?

Adeline, as they returned home through a romantic glen, when her senses were no longer absorbed in the contemplation of this grand scenery, and when its images floated on her memory only in softened colors, repeated the following lines:

SUNRISE

A Sonnet

Oft let me wander, at the break of day,
  Thro' the cool vale o'erhung with waving woods;
Drink the rich fragrance of the budding May,
  And catch the murmur of the distant floods,
Or rest on the fresh bank of limpid rill,
  Where sleeps the violet in the dewy shade,
Where opening lilies balmy sweets distill,
  And the wild musk-rose weeps along the glade.

Two pages farther on, Adeline

as she viewed the tranquil splendor of the setting sun ... touched the strings of the lute in softest harmony, her voice accompanying it with words which she had one day written after having read that rich effusion of Shakespeare's genius, "A Midsummer Night's Dream."

I omit the lines from Titania to her Lover, but take up the thread immediately after them.

Adeline ceased to sing — when she immediately heard repeated in a low voice,

"To mortal sprite such dulcet sounds,
  Such blissful hours, were never known!"

and turning her eyes whence it came, she saw M. Armand. She blushed and laid down the lute, which he instantly took up, and with a tremulous hand drew forth tones

"That might create a soul under the ribs of Death."

In a melodious voice, that trembled with sensibility, he sang the following sonnet.

We may also pass over the sonnet, which led M. Armand to burst into tears, and come to the sunset in the next chapter. As she observed it,

Adeline, resigning herself to the luxury of sweet and tender emotions, repeated the following lines.

All that we need of the lines is their closing couplet:

So sweet! so tranquil! may my evening ray
Set to this world — and rise in future day.

After which:

Adeline quitted the heights, and followed a narrow path that wound to the beach below: her mind was now particularly sensible to fine impressions, and the sweet notes of the nightingale, amid the stillness of the woods, again awakened her enthusiasm.

And the poem "To the Nightingale" ends:

Then hail, sweet bird! and hail *thy pensive tear*
To taste, to fancy, and to virtue dear!

Now Adeline's prompt responsiveness to stimulus is typical. Your sentimentalist, if I may risk a most unsentimental simile, is very like a penny-in-the-slot machine. Let nature drop in a sunset, or life a heart-throb, there is a little click, and a poem drops soft and warm into your outstretched hand. Why not? The austere requirements of clarity of imagery, of precision and lucidity of thought, of compression and balanced harmony of form — these trouble the sentimentalist not a whit. All that is necessary is to reach out into an atmosphere of rosy mist, and capture the first nebulous notion that floats into one's grasp. If it is the pensive tear of a nightingale, the absence of lachrymatory glands in that otherwise poetic bird is beneath the notice of the divine afflatus. The sentimentalist escapes the stern travail of thought. The poem is born in a sort of poetic twilight sleep.

"The greatness of an author," wrote George Henry Lewes in an infinitely suggestive little book, "The Principles of Success in Literature," — "consists in having a mind extremely irritable, and at the same time steadfastly imperial." The artist, in other words, must be sensitive and receptive to impressions, alert to every stimulus from within and from without, beyond the capacity of ordinary men. But he must hold imperial sway over his impressions, selecting,

clarifying, ordering, moulding, filing, and re-
filing them. The sentimentalist is often enough
extremely irritable, in Lewes's sense; he is never
steadfastly imperial. Impressions flow through
him and drop on us. "To sit as a passive bucket
and be pumped into," says Carlyle of Coleridge's
talk, "can in the long run be exhilarating to no
creature, how eloquent soever the flood of utterance that is descending." And poetry which bathes
us in lukewarm emotion is not toughening to the
spiritual fibre.

I wish we could think that such poetry has
sometimes a certain value as a sort of propæ-
deutic for the primary grades. The heart of the
crowd is undoubtedly a thing of vague, inchoate
yearnings to be touched. It may be more or less
distressing, but it is none the less significant,
that it is the sentimental doggerel sung by two
lovers in the spotlight during every comic opera
that draws the most heartfelt and continuous
applause. And on a little higher plane, we know
the audience that has tears to shed, and throngs
to shed them, over "Camille," and the "Music-
Master." And there are also gospel hymns. If
one could believe that the fondness for the sentimental song were the protoplasm of a liking for
"Tristan and Isolde," and that the far-off interest

of the tears shed over "Camille" were a capacity
for the purging through pity and fear afforded by
"Othello" or "King Lear," the case would be
a reasonably clear one. But I fear that evolution
does not so work. A taste formed on the cloying
sweetness of the sentimental is more apt than
not to turn away unfed from the stern sweetness
— Montaigne's "sévère douceur" — of great
poetry.

Happily, the great English tradition has kept
its sweetness sound and wholesome. Sentimental
verse in English, appalling as its expanse may be,
represents a back-water, past which the main
stream flows fresh and strong. Sentimentality,
however automatically it may exude itself in
verse, is not and cannot be the stuff of poetry.
And that is our salvation.

I have dealt now with the emphasis of the
poetic tradition in English on actions and ideas,
and with its relations to didacticism and sentimentality. I do not wish to close this course
without a word as to the spirit of English poetry,
as that spirit concerns us now.

These lectures have been written with a di-
vided mind. Why talk about poetry with a
world in flames? Is there not poignant truth once
more in those words which Carlyle wrote in his

"Life of Sterling": "As to song so-called ... we will talk of that a couple of centuries hence, when things are calmer again. Homer shall be thrice welcome; but only when Troy is *taken:* alas, while the siege lasts and battle's fury rages everywhere, what can I do with Homer?" That comes home with pitiless directness to any one who ventures to talk of poetry to-day.

And yet if poetry is, as I believe it to be, not merely an ornament that graces life, but an intimate reading and record of life, as life strives to catch and fix in form the endless flux in which it moves — if poetry is life itself, reaching out creatively after the permanence of beauty — then poetry is worthy of consideration now. Shelley wrote in his "Defence of Poetry" these profoundly suggestive words:

We want the creative faculty to imagine that which we know; we want the generous impulse to act that which we imagine; we want the poetry of life: our calculations have outrun conception; we have eaten more than we can digest. The cultivation of those sciences which have enlarged the limits of the empire of man over the external world, has, for want of the poetical faculty, proportionally circumscribed those of the internal world; and man, having enslaved the elements, remains himself a slave. . . .

The cultivation of poetry is never more to be desired than at periods when, from an excess of the selfish and calculating principle, the accumulation of the materials of external life exceed the quantity of the power of assimilating them to the internal laws of human nature.

That selfish and calculating principle has taken a form, in these days in which we are both privileged and doomed to live, which Shelley, I think, could scarcely have conceived, — the form of a national and racial egoism that has turned a continent into a shambles. I do not believe that poetry is a panacea for the cataclysm of a world; I should be ashamed to regard it as a sentimental refuge, a fugitive and cloistered retreat from the most tremendous issues that humanity has ever faced. If there is in it a tonic virtue, an assurance that the stuff of our stock is indestructible, that, at least, justifies our concern with poetry now. Heaven forbid that I should seem to preach or sentimentalize. But the spirit that animates our race to-day is the spirit that has animated English poetry itself from those earliest days when its virile speech, unintelligible now, embodied the same indomitable will that yet looks on tempests and is never shaken.

Gaston Paris, at the beginning of the Franco-Prussian war, lectured at the Collège de France on the "Chanson de Roland." No man ever brought to the study of poetry a more sternly scientific attitude, or a more rigorous devotion to truth, than that master of method in research. And what he pointed out in his opening lecture was this: the spirit of France — that gallant and chivalrous spirit that has streamed like an oriflamme through the storms of centuries — was implicit in that old masterpiece. He could not know that this same spirit would later find its apotheosis in the magnificent "They shall not pass" of Verdun. And what I want to make clear is the fact that the "Carry on" of England and America has been present in English poetry from its beginnings. For poetry is not something isolated and aloof from life, a fit subject merely for tea-table talk, or even doctoral dissertations. It is these things, and rightly; but it is more. It is the incarnation of the spirit of a people.

From its very beginnings English poetry has embodied a superb individualism. We say we are fighting to make the world safe for democracy. I do not know fully what that means; I wish I did. But if it means anything vital and constructive, it must include the conservation of the spirit of the race. And that spirit, whatever the checks and balances upon excess, has been uncompromisingly individualistic. Not only is it the individual who has dreed his own weird, but it has been the individual who has moulded the inert mass. Now great poetry is never written *à parti pris*, and its interpretation of the temper of a great people is implicit, not dogmatic or express. And a poetry that numbers among its preëminent figures Beowulf, and Chapman's Bussy d'Ambois, and Milton's Satan and Samson Agonistes, and Tennyson's Ulysses, and Childe Roland, who to the Dark Tower came, is a poetry whose democracy is tempered by a stubborn conviction that democracy thwarts the development of the individual at its peril.

Let me be still more concrete and specific. For I want to make clear, as one of the things which poetry has to offer to-day, a continuity of tradition that runs from the battle of Maldon to Ypres and Arras and the Somme. In that fine old Anglo-Saxon poem, the "Battle of Maldon," a veteran warrior, when the tide was setting strong against a dwindling handful, speaks to his young comrades in arms:

> Hige sceal þe heardra, heorte þe cenre,
> mod sceal þe mare, þe ure maegen lytlað.

"Purpose shall be the sterner, heart the bolder, courage the more, as our strength littleth." I wish I might quote the whole poem. Nothing that

has yet come from this vast carnage touches it
for stern beauty. Yet, barring the accidents of
changed conditions, it might have been written
yesterday. So might the words of the hero of the
old romance, "Libeaus Desconus":

> As he gan sore smerte,
> *Up he pullede hys herte,*
> And keverede of hys state.

"When pain smote him sore, up he pulled his
heart, and was himself again." It's like Johnie
Armstrong in the ballad:

> Said John, Fight on my merry men all,
> I am a little hurt, but I am not slain;
> I will lay me down for to bleed a while,
> Then I'll rise and fight with you again.

It is the same dauntlessness that animates Milton's splendidly English Satan:

> What though the field be lost?
> All is not lost — the unconquerable will,
> And study of revenge, immortal hate,
> And courage never to submit or yield,
> And what is else not to be overcome.

It animates Ulysses, as Ulysses, in a new Odyssey, passed from Homer by way of Dante into
English poetry:

> Tho' much is taken, much abides; and tho'
> We are not now that strength which in old days
> Moved earth and heaven, — that which we are, we are,

> One equal temper of heroic hearts,
> Made weak by time and fate, but strong in will
> To strive, to seek, to find, and not to yield.

And "Prospice" and "Childe Roland" and "The Grammarian's Funeral" and the Epilogue to "Asolando" need no quotation here.

Moreover, English poetry from its very beginnings is permeated by that dynamic fatalism which has characterized our stock. There is a fatalism (one thinks of the type as preëminently Oriental) which says: "What shall be, will be; why act?" — and folds its hands. There is another type which says: "What shall be, will be" — and leaps to action, hand in hand with fate. *Navigare necesse est, vivere non est necesse* — "sail we must, we need not live" — that motto, inscribed over the doorway of one of the great halls of the Hanseatic League, sums up the spirit. And that has been the fatalism of our Anglo-Saxon ancestry. You find it in "Beowulf":

> Wyrd oft nereð
> unfægne eorl, þonne his ellen deáh!

"Fate often saves an unfated warrior, *if his courage holds!*" And "Beowulf" is nowhere more consummately national than in that superb resolution of foreordination and free-will. Cromwell's "Put your trust in God, but mind to keep your

powder dry"; Franklin's "God helps those who
help themselves," are but other phrasings of the
same canny playing of the game with destiny.
You get it in one of the greatest of the old romances, the English "Gawain and the Green
Knight":

> Þe knyȝt mad ay god chere,
> & sayde, "quat schuld I wonde,
> Of destines derf & dere?
> *What may mon do bot fonde?"*

"The knight made ever good cheer and said: Why
should I swerve from destinies stern and strange?
What can one do but dare?" And Chaucer, in
that great balade in which he concentrates all that
the Middle Ages felt about Fortune—Chaucer
strikes the same ringing note:

> This wrecched worldes transmutacioun,
> As wele or wo, now povre and now honour,
> With-outen ordre or wys discrecioun
> Governed is by Fortunes errour;
> But natheles, the lak of hir favour
> Ne may nat don me singen, though I dye,
> *"Iay tout perdu mon temps et mon labour":*
> For fynally, Fortune, I thee defye!

The same indomitableness speaks again in Henley:

> I am the master of my fate:
> I am the captain of my soul.

And it is the moving spirit of the stark austerity of Thomas Hardy's verse, as it dominates his prose. And finally, the acceptance of fate as a call and not a *quietus*, finds expression in the superb close of Whitman's "Passage to India":

> Sail forth — steer for the deep waters only,
> Reckless O soul, exploring, I with thee, and thou
>   with me;
> For we are bound where mariner has not yet dared
>   to go,
> And we will risk the ship, ourselves and all.

The poetry which embodies the temper of our stock has tonic quality.

And the modern pedagogical psychologist asseverates that only contemporary poetry has fit place in the schools! If the inculcation of a long and glorious tradition, if familiarity with great spirit embodied in great form, be not an element of surpassing value in any education that is worthy of the name, then let us frankly recognize that in our concern with producing the efficiency of a machine, we are no longer interested in the making of men.

For that which goes to the making of great poetry is, *mutatis mutandis*, the law of the moulding of life. And I return in closing to the thesis with which this course began. Here is the individual, and here the chaotic welter of the life about him. And the object of the artist whose medium is words, and of that other artist whose medium is life, is one: it is to give to the amorphous welter *form*. Carlyle once said of Tennyson: "Alfred is always carrying a bit of chaos around with him, and turning it into cosmos." Well, that is poetry's job, and it is amazingly like the enterprise of life. And one reason why poetry is worthy of the consideration of men and women breathing thoughtful breath, in this return to chaos, is the fact that poetry's essence is also, in a sense that is profoundly true, the goal of life — it is creative energy made effective through restraint. And in these days when a shattered world is to be made over, and moulded into form and comeliness again, whatever throws into relief the eternal validity of the balance between freedom and restraint, of the belief that the individual is most truly individual when he builds, as individual, upon that which is common to him and to his kind — whatever lays stress on that, is of constructive worth. And that is why, in spite of what has seemed at times the almost unbearable triviality of all but the one overpowering fact, I have still ventured to deal with poetry.

THE END